THE
WHOLE FOODS
EXPERIENCE

2nd Edition

THE
WHOLE FOODS EXPERIENCE
Everybody's Guide to Better Eating
2nd Edition

by Ellen Sue Spicer-Jacobson

ROSS BOOKS

P.O. Box 4340 • Berkeley, California • 94704

Library of Congress Cataloging-in-Publication Data

Spicer-Jacobson, Ellen Sue.
The whole foods experience / Ellen Sue Spicer-Jacobson. -- 2nd ed. p. cm.
Includes bibliographical references and index.
ISBN 978-0-89496-021-5 -- ISBN 978-0-89496-030-7
1. Cookery (Natural foods) I. Title.
TX741.S665 2010
641.5'636--dc22
2010018830

Dedication

 This book is dedicated to my family. They lovingly shared my experience and experiments with whole foods.

Acknowledgements

This book would not have been possible without the conscientious assistance of Lynn Al-lopenna, the encouragement from free-lance editor Marsha Scott Gori, the quiet space given to me by my friends in Woodstock, New York, the introduction to my publisher by my writer-friend Fran Goulart, Franz Ross, my publisher, and Catherine Billey, my editor, who had faith in my work. I thank you all.

ISBN 978-0-89496-021-5 (Paper)
ISBN 978-0-89496-030-7 (eBook)

Cover by Martha Breen Bredemeyer.
Book design by Catherine Billey.
Illustrations by Linda Cook.
Typeset in Goudy Catalogue MT Std
Some title display in Palatino Linotype

Ross Books, P.O. Box 4340, Berkeley, CA 94704

Table of Contents

Introduction

If you can remember buying fresh, dark brown bread from the neighborhood bakery, crisp, just-picked produce from the truck farmer, and rich, whole milk from the corner grocery store, then basic foods are not strangers to you. Yet, several years ago, something happened to the simple, unadulterated food you and I grew up with: America entered the age of the supermarket. Now, up and down the wide, clean aisles, we're presented with an alarmingly large number of items never available, or even imaginable, to our mother's generation. Boxed, packaged, canned and frozen food sections of the food stores occupy more square footage than the fresh produce sections, and the sheer variety of ready-made meals makes dietary decision-making genuinely overwhelming.

Several years ago, I started to question many of the items sold as food in supermarkets. Reading labels, I realized that a lot of the things I was feeding my family contained artificial additives and preservatives, extenders, emulsifiers and chemicals with names I couldn't spell or even pronounce. I began to do a little research on these "wonder" ingredients, and finally came to the conclusion that most of them were of questionable value. I knew that my family's health was too important to be jeopardized by food products that were worthless, if not dangerous, so I reached a decision: I was going to stick with pure, basic food in my home. We didn't need artificial color or imitation flavor. We needed real food—whole foods.

Fortunately, my decision to get back to basics coincided with a small revolution taking place in many supermarkets. Americans have become health- and nutrition-conscious, and the store owners and food companies are responding. For instance: shoppers can now buy fruits and vegetables canned in their own juices—minus the salt, sugar, and preservatives. Most supermarkets now contain Health and Natural food sections. Consumers are becoming more and more aware of the link between diet and disease, and are demanding real food—whole foods. Oh yes, the junk is still there, but the good stuff is slowly and surely regaining its foothold on the shelves of our neighborhood stores. Whole foods are definitely back in style, and I think they are here to stay!

Now you're probably thinking: "Fine, so now I can get it, but once I get it, what do I do with it?" We've grown so accustomed to the ease of serving processed and prepared foods that making real food has come to seem difficult and mysterious. Take heart; it's easier, and a lot more fun, than you might think. The extra time you invest is paid back a thousand-fold, not only by increased health for you and your family but by the sheer *pleasure* of cooking real food: crisp vegetables, juicy, fragrant fruits, and (best of all) the wonderful experience of kneading and baking your own fresh bread. Whole food looks, smells, and tastes better than any chemical concoction you can buy in a cardboard box.

Perhaps you're already a convert and you don't need much coaxing yourself, but you're discouraged or skeptical about convincing your family to give up potato chips and candy. I admit, it's not always easy, but it *can* be done, and it's well worth the effort. You can imagine my satisfaction when my young daughter sat down in front of a freshly tossed salad she had made herself and exclaimed: "This is my salad and I can't wait to eat it!" Or when my son, a fussy eater, paused while eating a peanut butter and celery snack to peek at the stove and say: "Good, you made steamed broccoli!"

Where did I start? Certainly not by tossing out all the canned foods, the sugared cereals, and the "juices" with only 10 percent real fruit juice, in one fell swoop. If you want to establish good nutrition habits, you must set up a gradual plan—and may have to even be a bit sneaky. Ease your family into healthy new eating habits while encouraging the old ones to die slowly and gracefully. If you stumble once in a while, don't feel guilty. An occasional "junk binge" is par for the course during this learning period. If your children are old enough to respond actively to your new project, talk to them about your ideas and invite them to help you. Explain that you want them to have strong bones and teeth, clear skin, and healthy, happy bodies. You might just be surprised by their reaction to real food.

Although nutrition is only one aspect of good health, it is an area in which you and your family can play a powerful role. Any and all advances toward wholesome eating habits are worthwhile. Take things one step at a time, and when you find your toddler prefers a carrot to candy, your nine-year-old munches on fruit instead of fried chips, your teenager crunches pumpkin seeds instead of pretzels, and your spouse sips iced herbal tea instead of sugary soda, you'll know you've helped your family develop a happier, healthier life style.

Chapter One

Getting Started

You *could* stage a "spring cleaning". You could open your kitchen cabinets and propel all those packages containing while flour, white sugar, artificial additives, preservatives and salt in the general direction of the trash can. You could throw out all the questionable non-foods, like coffee and non-herbal tea. You could junk the junk food: chocolate bars, potato chips, soda, donuts, chemical ice cream (with very little real cream) and frozen fruit juices with no real fruit. And you *could* have mutiny in the kitchen. Not to mention a collapsed budget.

Radical approaches to changing your family's diet may be quick, but they're not easy—and they're certainly not necessary. I was able to make gradual changes without too many complaints from my children. My husband was my greatest ally. He supported me all the way, and often encouraged me to continue my nutritional quest when I became discouraged. He sampled all the new foods with enthusiasm and was the most powerful underlying force in helping me make the changes I felt were necessary. The children soon realized that both their parents were genuinely concerned about their good health.

The Altman Basic Four

I began with a new Basic-Four food grouping as my guide. This is not the "Basic Four" proposed by the United States Department of Agriculture 21 years ago, which replaced a former Basic Seven and an even earlier Basic Twelve. Rather, it is a revised Basic Four formulated by nutrition-writer Nat Altman. His plan from an article in Vegetarian Times (Jan.-Feb., 1977), provided me with excellent, helpful information. You can use these groupings—and this book— to help you make the switch over to whole foods. Begin with any group and gradually incorporate the natural alternatives from that group into your daily diet as you eliminate the less nutritious, highly processed foods you're eating now.

Protein Group

Emphasis is on non-meat proteins like nuts, seeds, and legumes (e.g. peas, beans, and lentils).

In the protein group, begin to replace processed cheese with whole, natural, unpreserved cheese. Use only plain yogurt instead of sugar-sweetened yogurt; add fresh fruit for sweetness. Consider reducing the amount of meat from your table and try substituting some legumes, nuts, seeds, and soy products.

Heavy meat consumption has been linked with several diseases — cancer being one of them. Many Americans are beginning to re-evaluate the role meat, especially red meat, plays in their meal planning. For a close up on the beef problem in relation to disease, I recommend Chapter 5 of "The Beef-Up Animal Machine", from Beatrice Trum Hunter's revealing book Consumer Beware (see bibliography). Synthetic and contaminated animal feed, antibiotics, poor inspection procedures and breeding practices are shown to lead to such minor problems as nausea and diarrhea and such major afflictions as breast cancer, male sterility, and arrested growth in children. Problems with poultry and fish are also discussed in Ms. Hunter's book on the over processing of our food.

Vegetable Group

Green and yellow leafy vegetables, carrots, onions, radishes, and sprouts (seeds and grains germinated in water and used in salads and sandwiches—a good source of vitamins, minerals, and chlorophyll).

Try to use more fresh "veggies" along with the canned and frozen kinds you may normally buy. Learn to steam your fresh vegetables instead of cooking them in water. Take a little extra time to sprout your own seeds and grains. It's fun, economical, and very healthy. This may mean some slight changes in your timing when you're preparing meals, but the resulting nutritive value of fresh, raw or lightly steamed vegetables and fresh sprouts in salads is well worth a few adjustments.

*F*ruit Group
Fresh, whole fruit and whole fruit juice with special attention to those providing Vitamin A and Vitamin C.

While you may already be giving some fresh fruit to your children for lunch or snacks, think about using fruit as a complete meal. If you are buying fruit juice drinks, switch to real fruit juices. Mix the fruit drinks with real unsweetened fruit juice until you wean your children away from the extra-sweet taste. Eventually serve only pure fruit juices; those without added sugar or honey. While honey is more acceptable as a natural sweetener, the fruit flavor of juices is naturally sweet and needn't be altered. Eventually cut down on juices altogether since they are a very concentrated form of fruit. Eat the whole fruit instead.

*E*nergy/Fiber Group
Whole grain breads, cereals, brown rice; also includes starchy vegetables like potatoes.

Consider a gradual elimination of white bread, white pasta, and white rice from your diet. These do not provide the necessary fiber for normal elimination (see Dr. Denis Burkett's Eat Right to Stay Healthy and Enjoy Life More). White flour has been stripped of the important layers of bran that aid proper digestion. Vitamin and protein-rich wheat germ, and some 22 other nutrients, are removed from the wheat kernel during sifting, bleaching, and other processes performed in commercial flour mills. The manufacturer then adds three synthetic B vitamins, vitamin D, and iron, and calls the white bread enriched. "This is impoverished flour, not enriched!" says Avelyn Bruce in her article entitled "Whole Foods vs. Empty Calories" (Today's Chiropractic, July-Aug. 1981).

If you cannot bake your own whole grain bread, then purchase bread made from whole wheat, rye, or oats, without the unnecessary additives, preservatives, and coloring agents found in commercial breads. Learn to read labels and make intelligent, wholesome choices. Real, fresh, natural bread contains no preservatives, so store it in your freezer or refrigerator to avoid mold and breakdown.

Whole grain pasta has become available in some supermarkets as they respond to consumer demands. Try different kinds until you find one your family enjoys. There are corn noodles, whole wheat mixed with sesame, spinach spirals and soy noodles that look almost like white noodles if you want to "fool" your family for awhile.

Brown rice looks and tastes a little different when you're used to white. Try mixing some brown with the white, camouflaged with sauces at first if necessary, until white rice begins to taste like paste to your kids' mouths and they start to clamor for the heartier brown.

Next, campaign to replace the heavily sugared breakfast cereals with more wholesome substitutes. A few large companies have come out with sugarless or low sugar cereals, but still use salt. So why not make your own? Granola is fun to prepare and one of the children can do it with minimal supervision or, better yet, make it a family project. Gradually reduce the amount of sweetener in the recipe until you have a granola that is naturally sweet from the toasted grains, nuts and dried fruit.

Replace highly processed fiber foods with whole foods. There's no reason to use mealy, instant mashed potato flakes when real ones not only taste better but are more nutritious as well. Instant foods lose much of their nutritive value and fiber content and are far inferior to their natural counterparts. Eventually, you'll find yourselves choosing a simple baked or steamed potato. You won't have to overcook, mash, and generally mutilate these and other complex carbohydrate foods like beets, squash, cauliflower and sweet potatoes.

*P*atience and Perseverance

Plain, real food will begin to look and taste as good as it naturally is. When you decide to follow the Basic Four group method, your meals may be out of focus, or even rather schizo, at first. Understand that the process of change is uneven. You may send your child to school with a processed cheese spread on whole wheat bread. Or you might continue using your family's favorite sugar-laced syrup on your new, whole grain pancakes. When fixing fruit salad, you might find canned peaches right alongside fresh apple slices or sugar-sweetened canned juice blended with real apple juice. White spaghetti and commercial sauce may be served with a fresh salad and homemade desserts without sugar.

Relax—little by little your cabinets will have fewer and fewer products with preservatives, sugar, additives, and whatever the latest carcinogen happens to be. You may not give up that morning cup of coffee for a couple of years, but have patience. The remnants of the typical American diet will eventually disappear along with the "typical" colds and flu that we generally accept as normal.

In the beginning, your children might be embarrassed to take their whole wheat bread sandwiches to school. Alfalfa sprouts in their sandwiches and dried fruit tucked into a brown bag lunch may seem strange to the other kids at first. Hang on! After some time passed, my own children became confident that their diet was the best one, and they lost their initial insecurity. Now they feel sorry for the kids whose parents pack lunches made of fluffy white bread sandwiches, sugary cookies, and imitation chocolate milk.

One final word of warning: don't push your children or yourself too quickly. Highly processed foods are generally loaded with salt, sugar, and artificial flavors which overpower the true taste of food. For some members of the family, natural foods may not be as tasty at first as their processed counterparts. While you are struggling with how to buy and prepare foods differently, your family is adjusting to new taste sensations and combinations. Immediate depletion of such things as sugar can sometimes result in painful, even severe, withdrawal symptoms. Radical changes of diet will not benefit you physiologically, so beware of attempting too much, too soon.

Natural foods will soon taste superior. My own kids now prefer the taste of real fruit, raw vegetables, dark bread, unsulfured dried fruit, and generally plainer foods. Their skin is clearer, their teeth are cavity-free, and they don't suffer from excessive colds or bouts of flu. While they have always had fresh air, rest, sunshine and exercise (all contributors to good health) it was not until I changed to a more natural diet that I noticed a real improvement in their overall health.

Just remember to introduce each new food positively and lovingly. A slow easing into natural foods is much more gratifying than the old sink-or-swim technique. My early dietary changes were encouraged by a naturapath, Avron Kartyshai, who told me to pin the words "Patience" and "Perseverance" on my refrigerator door—which I did. No two words can better describe the attitude necessary to start a typical, junk-eating American family on the road to a wholesome diet.

Beginner's List for a Natural Foods Kitchen

For an organized start, listed here are some simple change-over foods within each of Airman's four categories:

Protein Group
Natural peanut butter made only with peanuts

Raw milk from cows or goats; also nut milk or soybean milk

Eggs from hens that run loose, eat natural feed, and are allowed to mate

Natural cheese without preservatives, preferably raw milk cheese

Homemade yogurt or quality-brand commercial yogurt with nothing artificial or added

Vegetable Group
Canned vegetables without salt in lead-free tins, or home canned vegetables without salt

Frozen vegetables without salt as well as dehydrated vegetables

Fresh vegetables and sprouts (try to get unsprayed)

Fruit Group
Fruit packed in water, not syrup

Fresh fruit (try to get it unsprayed)

Sun-dried fruits packaged without chemicals, naturally dark and chewy

Energy-Fiber Group
Whole wheat flour and other whole grains for baking

Whole grain breads without additives or preservatives

Brown rice

Granola (homemade with little sweetener), familia (raw oats, nuts, and raisins), unsweetened cereals without preservatives

Non-instant oatmeal and other hot cereals made from whole grains

(Raw fruits and vegetables are also good fiber sources.)

Chapter Two

The World of Whole Foods

For a long time I shopped only in the supermarket. I think the long aisles of familiar foods gave me a feeling of security. When I finally did venture into a natural foods store, I was pleasantly surprised by the homey atmosphere and helpful staff. Label reading was simpler; less fraught with pitfalls. For many people, shopping at a whole foods store for the first time can be an exhilarating experience. I once heard a woman exclaim as she first walked into a natural foods store: "This is a whole other world!" And whole is the key word.

Try to select a shop that has jars, barrels, or transparent packages so you can poke around and putter about, learning more about the new foods you want to use. Pick a store where you feel comfortable browsing and asking questions. Feel free to buy only a few items in small amounts. You may want to start with the natural section of a supermarket, since many new supermarkets now have entire sections devoted to whole foods.

My favorite store is the kind that has bulk items in barrels or large ceramic containers, so I can buy as much, or as little, as I like. Since packaging is a big business (costly in both labor and materials), purchasing in bulk will actually save you money. Another advantage to bulk buying is that most stores turn over their stock fairly quickly to avoid spoilage. Boxed grains can sit on a supermarket shelf for several months before being purchased, so do buy in bulk whenever possible. Start collecting jars for your new natural food items, and you'll soon have a colorful cupboard full of grains, beans, noodles, nuts and other good foods.

It's important to have a positive, adventurous attitude towards what you find. Many people sneer at the unfamiliar or reject it without a fair trial. Cynicism and reluctance never work, especially if you are sincere about improving your family's diet. You don't have to accept every new item you see, but you should be open to new ideas in recipe preparation, and try a new food more than once before striking it from your list.

To become a discriminating natural foods shopper, make a list of the foods you wish to try based on the recipes in this book or other natural foods cookbooks you have discovered (carrying recipes with you is a big help). Buy one or two of the food items in small amounts as you need them and prepare the dish using your recent purchases. Watch for the foods your family likes best and which seem the most nutritious to you. As you learn how to use a "strange" new ingredient in other ways, it will become a regular item on your shopping list and will find a permanent place on your kitchen shelf or in your refrigerator.

Natural Foods List

Once you have found a fully stocked natural foods store with a friendly environment and helpful people, you are ready to explore the world of real food. Here's a list of the new foods you'll probably encounter, categorized as you're likely to find them in a natural foods store. All items you purchase should come from organic or unsprayed farms.

Whole Grains and Flours

The whole kernel of wheat, rye, oats, millet, buckwheat, and rice are categorized under whole grains. Pearled barley and couscous are not technically whole grains even though they are found in a natural foods store. You can use them as you move towards a whole grain diet, but use them sparingly. In the beginning, you may want to try unbleached white flour. Add the whole grains to the lighter flour gradually, until refined flour is used minimally, if at all.

Whole grain items are ground from the entire kernel. When the grain is completely ground, it is called a flour; when it is more coarsely ground, it is called a "meal"; when it is cut or chopped it is called a "grit" or "cracked cereal". Therefore, you can purchase whole wheat, rye, triticale, buckwheat, corn, millet, and oat flours, along with buckwheat grits, cracked wheat, cracked millet, corn meal, and so forth. Different recipes call for different forms of the grain and allow for a great variety of textures and tastes.

Breads

Natural foods stores carry an abundance of delicious whole grain breads. You can usually pick from whole wheat, cracked wheat, rye, and mixed grains, as well as whole wheat buns and rolls. If your children object to the darker breads at first, introduce them gradually. Try grilled cheese sandwiches or French toast to camouflage the difference. Use any subversive technique that works. If you try baking your own bread, choose from the variety of grains in the flour section; likewise when preparing cookies and muffins. Again, you may want to start with unbleached white flour and gradually add whole wheat flours. By keeping some of your traditional white bread and cakes along with the slowly accumulating whole wheat products, you might find better acceptance of the darker, chewier breads.

Crackers

Most natural foods stores and supermarkets with natural food sections carry a tasty line of whole grain crackers—rye, whole wheat, rice, cornmeal—without sugar, artificial flavor, or chemical preservatives. If the store is a good one, it should also have some salt-free crackers. Ask the owner to order some if you don't see any. Always try to omit the salt, even sea salt. Our daily salt needs are satisfied by the foods in a proper diet. Too much salt is linked with high blood pressure and other health problems. As you learn to enjoy the taste of pure, unadulterated food, the salt-free crackers will taste better and better.

Cold Cereals

Puffed cereals and granola-type cereals are commonly found in a natural foods store, but check the ingredients to see that sugar and salt is omitted. Granola is notorious for being overly sweet, and "natural" brands are no exception. The best cereals contain no artificial preservatives or colorings and should be made with whole grains and other basics such as unsalted nuts or seeds, unsprayed dried fruit, and unsweetened coconut.

Hot Cereals

Hot cereals are a warm and nutritious way to start off the day, especially on a cold, winter morning. Look for hot cereals that are made from whole grains; often a natural foods store will have bins of oatmeal or multi-grain cereals that are made of only the whole grain, and no extras. You prepare them "from scratch", but they take only a couple minutes more than their highly processed, quick-cereal, cousins. If your children are already used to pre-sweetened and refined quick cereals, mix in some unadulterated cereal of the same kind in their bowls, until they can be weaned away from their original brand. Stick with whole grains for nutrients and roughage, and avoid enriched versions; after the cereal has been milled, the enrichment process never replaces as much as it has removed.

Pasta/Noodles

While noodle products (in general) do not provide optimum nutrition because they are a processed food, they're almost always popular with kids, as well as adults. If you are going to make pasta products part of your meal planning, why not get the best nutrition for your food dollar?

Most natural food stores carry noodles made from whole wheat. Some stores sell whole wheat or mixed grain pastas in every size and shape, from alphabet soup noodles to ziti noodles. There are also corn ribbons, spinach lasagna or noodles, buckwheat (soba) noodles, and egg noodles in whole wheat, or wheat and soy, combinations.

Jerusalem artichoke noodles are another noodle category made from semolina, soy flour, and low-starch Jerusalem artichoke flour. They look like regular white noodles, but contain less starch. They are a good choice if your family really balks at green spinach or brown whole wheat noodles. You may want to start with Jerusalem artichoke products and work your way into the darker whole grain noodles. In any case, noodles are a processed food. So if you can, ease up on the pasta. You'll have fewer calories to worry about, as well.

Mixes

Several health-oriented food manufacturers sell "natural mixes," such as pancake or quick-bread mixes, instant freeze-dried dinners for use on camping trips, and premixed grains and spices for preparing complete casseroles. While these are clearly labeled as having no chemical additives or preservatives, many do contain salt, pepper and other ingredients you may eventually wish to avoid. Nevertheless, they are still superior in quality to commercial mixes. If you need a little food "insurance" for emergencies, natural mixes are better than the prepared kind.

Oils

Natural vegetable oils found in whole food stores are different from their commercial counterparts* The latter are treated with chemical solvents and caustic refining agents such as lye, harsh bleaching agents, deodorizing chemicals, and preservatives. The vegetable oils sold in natural foods stores are generally expeller-pressed (less heated), unbleached, un-deodorized, and unpreserved. Some are refined; others are not.

I suggest starting your family with a refined, natural oil, such as safflower. Then mix unrefined with refined, and eventually use only unrefined oils. These natural oils contain valuable nutrients such as chlorophyll, lecithin, Vitamin E, and minerals. Animal fats, such as chicken fat and lard, have no place in a natural foods diet. Neither do hardened vegetable oils, such as Spry or Crisco. All of these have been implicated as contributors to unhealthy arteries.

To get maximum nutritional benefits from different oils—sesame, walnut, olive, sunflower, peanut, and corn—use a variety over time. Each oil has its own special characteristics and can be used to enhance the flavor and texture of the foods you prepare. Once you have opened a bottle, keep it refrigerated, or in a very cool place, to prevent spoilage. Eventually, try to phase out heavy use of oils altogether, and use the whole foods from which the oils are made (e.g., saute in tomato juice instead of oil). After all, oil is a processed food.

Natural Sweeteners

A word of warning here: All sweeteners should be used sparingly—even honey. White refined sugar is primarily implicated in many dietary problems and behavior difficulties in children. But honey, maple syrup, sorghum, and others are sugars as well. If they must be included in your diet for the time being, look for unheated and unfiltered honey, barleycorn malt, molasses, pure maple syrup, and date "sugar." Each is unique in taste and texture, and they can all be substituted in varying amounts for white or brown sugar. As your children grow accustomed to less heavily-sweetened foods, you should be able to use less of even the natural sweeteners. For example, try substituting real fruit juice for sugar in baking.

Herbs and Spices

Some natural foods stores have an impressive inventory of herbs and spices for use in everything from food preparation to teas. However, some spices, such as black pepper or mustard, should be avoided or used sparingly, because they are irritants and tend to stimulate the appetite. Explore the world of spices yourself and make your own decisions, or consult a nutritionist. Cinnamon and Allspice are excellent for baking*; oregano, garlic, and thyme are essentially for cooking; and try cayenne, kelp, and dulse for salad seasoning. In any case, use cooking herbs and spices sparingly in order to enjoy the true taste of basic, whole foods. Herbs for teas also need to be investigated, since some can cause allergic reactions.

Legumes

This section includes dried beans and peas of every size and color: black-eyed peas, black turtle beans, lima beans, mung beans, navy beans, pinto beans, red kidney beans, soybeans (yellow and green), split peas (yellow and green), lentils (red and green), and chickpeas (garbanzos).

The best way to learn about their tastes and uses is to try experimenting with them, one or two at a time and in small amounts, and using them in soups, stews, salads, or dips. In their dry form, beans have a long shelf life. If a recipe calls for a specific bean, such as pintos for a Mexican dish, feel free to use another bean if pintos don't make a hit at mealtime. Garbanzo, lima, soy, and other beans can also be found in a variety of forms, including flours, flakes, and grits. Mix them with your whole grain flours or use them in place of some of the grains. The nutrients in these bean flours can nutritionally enhance your recipes, as well as improve and vary the tastes and textures of the results.

Nuts and Seeds

The variety of nuts and seeds available in any store depends on the popularity of the items and the size of the shop. Many places carry peanuts (actually a legume), sunflower seeds, pumpkin seeds, soy nuts, almonds, walnuts, brazil nuts, pecans, hazel nuts, and sesame seeds, all of which can be added to casseroles, breads and baked goods. (Alfalfa seeds, which are used mainly for sprouts, may be in this section or on the shelf with beans and seeds used especially for sprouting.) Sometimes you can find pistachios and pine nuts, but they are expensive and not always available in smaller stores.

Try to buy as many of the above as possible in their shells; they'll be fresher. If they aren't in their shells, at least purchase them unsalted and unroasted. Roasting accelerates the rate of rancidity, and salting is totally unnecessary and considered unhealthy. Unadulterated nuts are fun to eat and provide many valuable nutrients. Eat a variety for a fuller range of benefits, and store them in a cool place.

Dried Fruits

A selection of dried fruits is available in most stores. However, in a natural foods store, you should be able to choose from a selection of quality unsprayed and unsulfured fruit. You can choose from such fruits as apricots, peaches, papaya, persimmons, apples, pineapples, pears, dates, and figs. Honey-dipped and carob-coated dried fruits are also popular in natural food stores, but check to make sure they are not dried with sugar, or that the carob isn't laced with sugar.

Beverages

A quality natural foods store will carry a variety of unsweetened, and unaltered fruit and vegetable juices. Bottled juices are not as good as freshly squeezed juices, since almost all bottled juices are pasteurized before bottling to stop fermentation, destroying nutrients in the process. These beverages, however, are superior to the sweetened fruit drinks, filtered juices, and salted vegetable juices which still tend to dominate in the supermarket (check the natural foods section of the supermarket for unfiltered fruit and vegetable juices).

Hot beverages, such as herbal teas, carob, and grain-based coffee substitutes, are available in most health-oriented stores. These foods should contain no sugar or artificial ingredients.

Natural sparkling waters are often found in supermarkets as well as in natural foods stores. Use them to make a natural "soda," or drink them straight as a refreshing alternative to regular water. Don't forget to check labels to be sure the soda contains no questionable ingredients.

Spring water and distilled water are alternatives to tap water. There are many invisible ingredients in public drinking water that are questionable or harmful. Tap water should really only be used for bathing and rinsing off produce.

Dairy Produce

If your natural foods store has a cooler, you will be able to purchase quality yogurt, kefir, cottage cheese, butter, raw milk, margarine without chemicals, farm eggs, and natural hard cheese. Try to purchase raw milk (goat's or cow's) products; many nutritionists feel that pasteurized and/or homogenized milk products are robbed of important nutrients during processing.

Produce may also be found in the cooler. It should be unsprayed and grown organically on farms where the land has been cultivated without chemical fertilizers, the crops rotated, and the soil contains natural composted material. Certified organic produce means prices are usually a little higher, but you generally get a superior product.

Frozen foods are becoming more commonplace in many natural foods businesses. You can purchase unadulterated ice cream, frozen tofu ice cream, frozen yogurt, bread, frozen main and side dishes, as well as fruits and garden vegetables suitable for cold storage. Check ingredients on the labels to ensure a pure product. I do not believe ice cream belongs in a truly wholesome diet, but during a transition period, or for an occasional treat, it is acceptable.

Vitamins and Minerals

Almost every natural foods store carries dietary supplements. A health food store often devotes the most space in their shop to vitamins, although a natural foods store sells almost all food and only has a small vitamin/mineral section. In either store, the supplements should be organic, not synthetic, and you should choose the proper ones carefully. A nutritional

---

* If the child you will be feeding is hyperkinetic, I suggest that you use allspice rather than cinnamon in all recipes using cinnamon. I recently learned that cinnamon could be a problem to children with food sensitivities.

consultation might be valuable at this time.

Other Items

Other items found in natural foods stores include: wheat germ, nutritional yeast, miso paste, natural soy sauce, tofu, tahini, and many more exotic items you may want to eventually try. Start with the more familiar grains, beans, and flours, and work your way into the more unusual items. As the terms begin to grow familiar to you, add those you enjoy to your new list of foods. The challenge of creating new food tastes from wholesome ingredients will far outweigh any initial doubts you may have about experimenting with these unfamiliar items. The exciting world of natural foods awaits you, and all you have to do is take that first step into the store for your adventure to begin.

Chapter Three

Making Ends Meet Naturally

"I can't afford natural foods!"
"Natural foods put too big a dent in my food budget."
"Health foods are phony. You pay more for the same thing available in regular stores."

I'm sure you've heard one or all of these complaints before, but they aren't necessarily accurate. Yes, you can wind up spending a bundle on natural food, just as you can squander your entire budget on junk food. It's quite possible to save money with whole foods; all it takes is a little planning and some inside information. Here are three sound suggestions for buying natural foods that will help you stay within your budget:

a. Buy basic foods in bulk whenever possible — brown rice, beans, lentils, etc. Store in a cool, dry spot. Consider sharing with a friend if bulk buying sizes are too large.

b. Prepare your meals from scratch. This takes a bit longer, but once you become used to the basic techniques and the increasing benefits of your new, healthful diet, the time difference will be minor. Natural, prefabricated and fractioned, or fractured, food is easy to prepare and good for emergencies, but these convenience foods take the joy and creativity out of cooking.

c. Buy locally-grown food whenever possible. Farmers' markets and roadside stands usually offer good selections of seasonal foods at reasonable prices. Ask the farmer which produce is sprayed, and try to avoid those products. Consider growing sprouts, especially in the winter when lettuce prices are higher.

You can supplement your efforts at economical and nutritional buying with "ecological" cooking techniques like using leftovers in soups and stews, stretching meals with soy products, and cooking double the amount of grains for dinner and use to make another dish later. You may find that some natural foods cost more than their sprayed and refined counterparts; however, a whole diet consists of little, if any, expensive meat products, and this tends to balance the food budget. The whole foods that fill the protein gap left after the elimination of meats (i.e., grains and legumes) are much cheaper and more versatile, as well as healthier.

Some specific areas where you can save using the whole approach are:

a. Scoop-your own oats for hot and cold cereals vs. packaged oats (oatmeal).

b. Loose brown rice, bulghur, and other whole grains for cooking vs. prepackaged grains and grain dinners.

c. Loose, whole, dried beans (uncanned) vs. cellophane-packed beans and/or canned beans.

d. Whole sweet potatoes and white potatoes vs. their candied, flaked, and fried counterparts.

e. Whole, unsalted nuts vs. salted, oiled nuts.

f. Natural cheese cut from large wheels vs. pre-packaged, "natural cheeses". (Cheese food, or processed cheese, is an inferior product. While cheaper, it does not even qualify to be in the same category as real cheese.)

g. Unsliced, fresh, whole grain breads vs. commercially packed, pre-sliced, whole grain bread. (Whole grain breads are much chewier than their cottony counterparts; the actual loaf may have a higher cost, but you will probably be satisfied with eating less.)

h. Freshly ground (preferably home-ground) peanut butter without fillers or sweeteners vs. name-brand peanut butters of similar quality.

i. Individual frozen vegetables vs. combined vegetable dishes.

Where prices are higher, the quality should be higher as well. Raw foods are often slightly more expensive. A can of peaches may be cheaper than fresh peaches of equal weight minus the syrup, but "canned" means "loss of nutrients". Natural foods generally give you more for your budget dollar, especially when you learn to shop carefully. As you prepare complete meals from basic whole ingredients, you will find that the cost is significantly less. For example, preparing macaroni and cheese with whole wheat noodles and real cheese is cheaper than its pre-packaged counterpart. Of course, if you separately purchased white noodles and processed cheese to make the dish from scratch, it will cost even less, but it will also be almost worthless nutritionally. Beware of cheap food—it may be too cheap for your family's health.

Chapter Four

Essential Utensils

Cooking with natural foods does not always require completely new utensils. Many times the necessary equipment is already in your kitchen. Use this list to find new, natural foods uses for your old kitchen helpers.

Cooking Pots

Stainless steel pots are the safest (metal) for basic everyday cooking. Aluminum utensils are considered harmful. Aluminum leaching from pots and utensils into our food creates a potentially dangerous situation. While small amounts of the metal seem to be harmless, the effect is cumulative. The build-up of aluminum in the human body can eventually cause degeneration and disease. If you don't use stainless steel, then stick to uncoated, heavy gauge stainless, pyrex, enamel or cast iron. Some pots (even stainless steel) are made with aluminum cores for conducting heat. As long as the stainless steel covers the pot and the aluminum does not actually touch the food, I find no objection.

To serve a variety of meals, the following pots are essential:

a. Large Dutch oven, or similar flat based, wide diameter pot for stews and soups. Cast iron or stainless steel are the most practical.

b. Stainless steel vegetable steamer. This is one of the most essential pieces in the kitchen. I recommend buying two. The steamer can also be used to steam cold grains and to soften stale bread. If steamers are unavailable, use a colander that fits inside a large pot with a tight-fitting lid.

c. Two medium-sized, stainless steel saucepans, one with an inner liner to serve as a double boiler. A pyrex double boiler can be substituted for one of the steel pots.

d. One or two small stainless or enamel saucepans for miscellaneous needs. Be sure to buy a good quality enamel that won't chip easily.

e. Stainless steel or cast iron fry pan (10" -12" diameter). An electric fry pan is not necessary.

f. Small fry pan to saute vegetables. Cast iron preferred.

g. Two or three pieces of stove-to-table casserole dishes for meal-in-a-dish recipes or for serving grains and hot vegetables at the table.

h. Grater. A small table top grater will do most jobs perfectly well. Buy one made from stainless steel to avoid rusting. I have a wonderful, hand-cranked device with different heads for different food textures. The speed of a food processor makes for convenience, but it's not essential, unless your schedule is extremely busy.

i. Wooden spoons for mixing and stirring. One extra-long-handled spoon for mixing large pots of soup or reaching into the oven to stir grains.

j. One large stainless steel colander and one or two smaller strainers for draining and rinsing noodles, vegetables, fruits and grains.

B aking Equipment

If you plan to do some of your own bread, cake, and cookie baking, then a few bake pans are essential. Again, use stainless steel, tin, glass, or cast iron.

a. Two cookie sheets.
b. Two muffin tins.
c. Two or three regular size bread pans.
d. Two or three small bread pans for quick breads.
e. Two cake pans, round or square.
f. One large, oblong bake pan with high sides and lid to prepare grains or to make granola-like cereals. Can also double for lasagna or casserole pan.
g. Three or four mixing bowls, stainless or glass.
h. Measuring cups and spoons: one large pyrex measuring cup and one set of individual measuring cups or scoops. Small measuring spoons on a ring are also essential.
i. Rolling pin and bread board are important if you plan to make your own bread, pie crusts, and other pastry-type desserts or dishes.
j. Rubber or plastic spatulas and scrapers, one large and two or three smaller. Also, have a stainless steel spatula for turning pancakes or checking cookies in the oven.

Appliances

A few basic appliances are indispensible for the natural chef.

    a. Electric blender. Necessary for preparing drinks, baby foods, salad dressing, and some desserts.

    b. Wok. A cone-shaped Chinese cooking pot, excellent for making crisp, grease-free, stir-fried vegetables. It can also be used as a large base for steamers, as a utensil for preparing scrambled eggs, and for other dishes normally prepared in a flat pan.

    c. Electric seed and nut mill. A small but useful appliance that grinds nuts, seeds, and grains to a fine powder.

    d. A crock pot is helpful to have, especially if you work during the day or if you want to cook grains slowly at a low temperature (which prevents enzymes from being destroyed by high heat).

    e. Pressure Cooker. This is helpful for cooking grains and beans quickly although not as necessary as a steamer or wok.

Serving Dishes

I think whole food should look as good as it tastes, so attractive serving dishes are essential in my kitchen. Decorative and colorful wood, cut glass, china, or ceramic serving dishes make everyday meals a special occasion.

Salad bars are very popular in our household. You can arrange a variety of tempting fresh vegetables in various serving bowls and plates. Or try placing a big wooden bowl of tossed salad in the center of the table with smaller bowls of nuts, seeds, and other garnishes surrounding it.

Make use of your cookware as part of your dishware. For casseroles and other hot meals, move your decorated oven-to-table casseroles, a large soup tureen, or your wok right from the stove to the table at the time of serving. A truly distinctive serving dish frequently adds the final touch to a dinner table.

Even with all this equipment there is one essential utensil that cannot be ignored — you, the cook. If you bring enthusiasm and a good pair of willing hands into the kitchen, your meals will be easier to prepare, and more enjoyable to serve and to eat. A positive attitude is important in every aspect of life, and in the kitchen it can help create a warm, friendly atmosphere while you are working and when you serve your new creations. Good food can mean more than the actual quality of the food; it's the good feelings you have in presenting the food you have purchased and prepared with care and love.

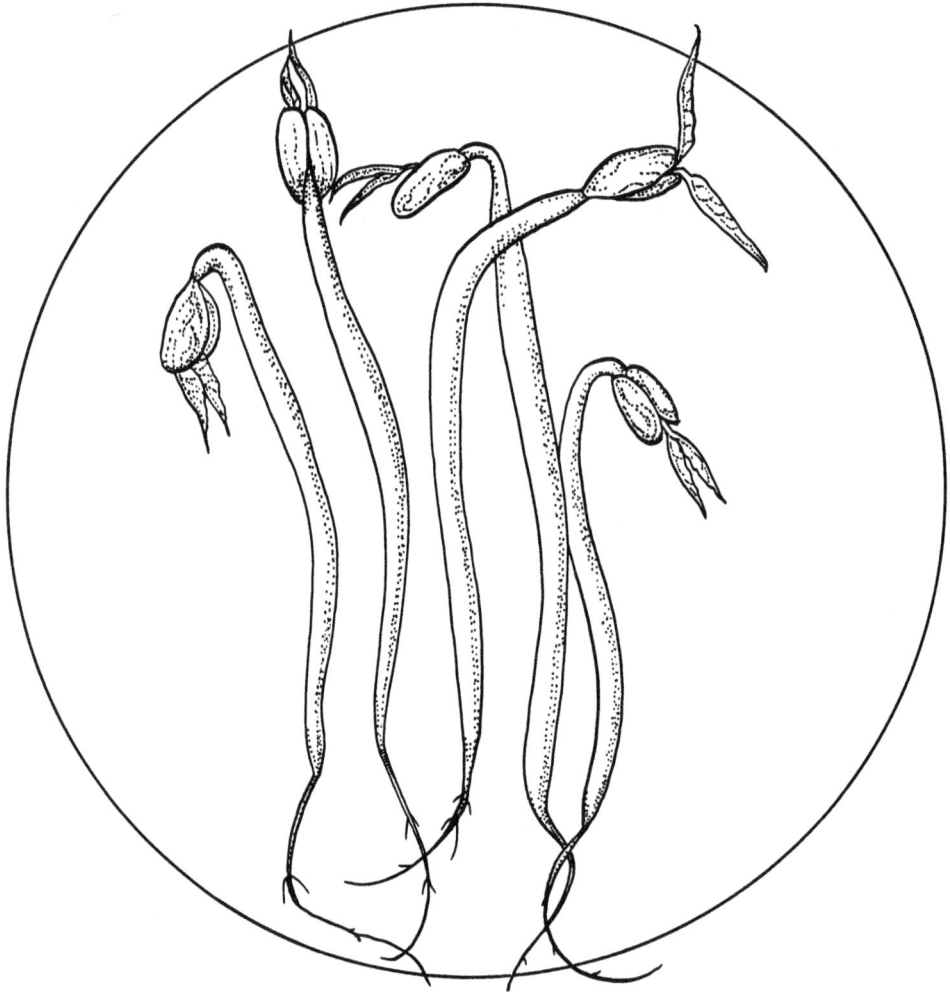

Chapter Five

Whole Hints

You may need some tips on how to handle and prepare the new whole foods that you've found in both the supermarket and the natural foods store. These materials will soon become familiar basics in both your cupboard and your daily cooking experience, but, until they do, a few hints are in order.

Dry Beans

Soak the beans in water overnight, covered. (Short cut: use a pressure cooker; follow manufacturer's instructions). Use plenty of water, since the beans expand. Drain beans the next day. Place on a cookie sheet in your freezer, separating beans as much as possible. When thoroughly frozen, cover and cook them in boiling water for about 1/2 hour. (Large beans may take a little longer.) Save water for stock. Place beans in refrigerator unless you plan to use them right away. (For flavorful stock, add carrots, onions, garlic, and celery to the bean water.)

This soaking, freezing, and cooking method cuts down on preparation time considerably. Unless you use a pressure cooker, this is the fastest method. Moreover, I often freeze a large batch of beans and remove them as I need them, cooking them while I prepare the rest of the casserole.

Sprouting

Sprouting is the simple process of growing grains, seeds, and beans on your kitchen counter. When the seeds are sprouted, they increase in nutritional value. They are rich in vitamins, minerals, and protein. By following these simple five steps, you will have sprouts in four or five days. You can use them for all your casseroles, as well as in soups, sandwiches, and salads.

1. Rinse and drain 1-2 Tablespoons of whole seeds or beans, and place in a wide-mouthed Jar. Cover with water for a few hours until seeds have swelled. (Alfalfa, about 4 hours, larger seeds and beans need about 8 hours.)

2. Cover the jar with cheese-cloth, nylon netting, wire mesh, or special sprouting lids. Rinse everything thoroughly with tepid water, pouring off excess. (Too much water causes rotting.)

3. Place jar on its side in your cupboard or on top of your counter (away from direct sunlight). The side position allows more growing space. If jar becomes "packed" with sprouts, divide between two jars to allow for proper growth.

4. Once or twice a day, rinse with cool—not cold—water (through the lid or in a sieve, removing the big seeds that aren't sprouting). Drain well and replace jar on its side.

5. Repeat process daily, and in 4-5 days sprouts will be ready. In about 5 days, alfalfa sprouts will become greener if you place them in the light after they are just sprouted. Wash, drain, and refrigerate. Try to use your sprouts within a week. If you don't use them right away, rinse them, and place in a clean jar in the refrigerator.

G rains

Listed below are the methods I find the best for cooking the different grains.

B arley (pearled)
Place one cup barley in two cups water or stock. Bring to a boil. Cover and cook over a low flame until all the water is absorbed and the grains are separate. You can also place the barley and water in an over proof dish and bake in a slow oven, adding vegetables of your choice for easy barley stew. (Unpearled, hulless barley* can be prepared by soaking overnight and cooking the next day until tender—very chewy.)

B rown Rice
Boil 2 cups of water for every 1 cup of rice. Add rinsed rice slowly to boiling water, and bring water to a second boil. Stir once, reduce heat, cover and simmer for about 35-40 minutes. Long grain rice takes longer than short or medium grain. Remove from stove and let sit a few minutes.

Buckwheat Groats (Kasha)

Toast 1 cup buckwheat groats in 350° oven for 10-15 minutes in an ungreased pan. (If groats are already purchased toasted, omit this step.)

Boil 2 1/2 - 3 cups water or stock and slowly add to the toasted groats. Mix, cover, and bake until all the water is absorbed, and the grains are dry and separate, approximately 15-20 minutes, depending on whether you use whole or cracked groats. You can add minced garlic and onions for added flavor. When grains are completely cooked, add soy sauce or spices of your choice.

Bulghur (toasted cracked wheat)

Pour two cups boiling water or stock over one cup bulghur and let water be absorbed. Keep warm in oven or stir-fry quickly in a fry pan, adding spices and vegetables of your choice. Can also be eaten as a cold grain with minced vegetables, oil, and lemon juice, known as tabouli (see recipe on p. 79).

Millet

Bring 4 cups of water or stock to a boil. Slowly add one 1 whole or cracked millet. Stir, reduce heat to low, cover, and let cook until all the water is absorbed (about 1 hour). Millet can also be prepared like kasha. (Pre-soaked or cracked millet takes less time.)

Grains & Beans: Creative Uses

a. For variety and nutrition, mix 2 or 3 grains when making a casserole (e.g. rice and millet, buckwheat and rice, bulghur and buckwheat, couscous and bulghur and rice).

b. Mix cooked, chilled rice or kasha (toasted buckwheat) with minced salad veggies and salad dressing for a tasty summer grain salad. Cooked beans add color and nutrition (e.g. pinto, black-eyed peas, black turtle beans, red kidney).

c. Puree warm, just-cooked beans with small amount of liquid from cooking the beans. Add tomato puree, herbs and spices for a quick bean spread.

d. Puree cooked beans and add to burger recipes, soups, and sauces.

---

* Available from Walnut Acres, Penns Creek, PA 17862.

e. Mix cooked grains and beans with your favorite spices and herbs, and use as a taco topping, pepper stuffing, or as a side dish in place of potatoes.

f. Add cooked beans to your favorite noodle dish (hot or cold) for interesting taste and texture.

g. Stir in extra grains or beans to a thin soup to make it thicker, or use grains and beans alone with a soup broth for simple soup.

h. Freeze leftover cooked grains or beans and use for future soups or casseroles.

i. Add sliced onions and peppers to chilled beans (2 or 3 together), toss with salad dressing and enjoy a hearty bean salad. For Mexican flair, add lightly cooked (not mushy) corn kernels.

j. Puree cooked beans and add to soup stock as a thickening agent or as a way to make soup creamier without the cream.

k. Toss warm cooked beans with steamed vegetables for vegetable variety (e.g. cauliflowerettes with kidney beans, broccoli with navy beans, carrots with black-eyed peas, green beans with kidney beans, corn with green soybeans, etc.).

l. Roast large beans like soy or garbanzo (already cooked); toss with dash of oil and herbs and use as munchies.

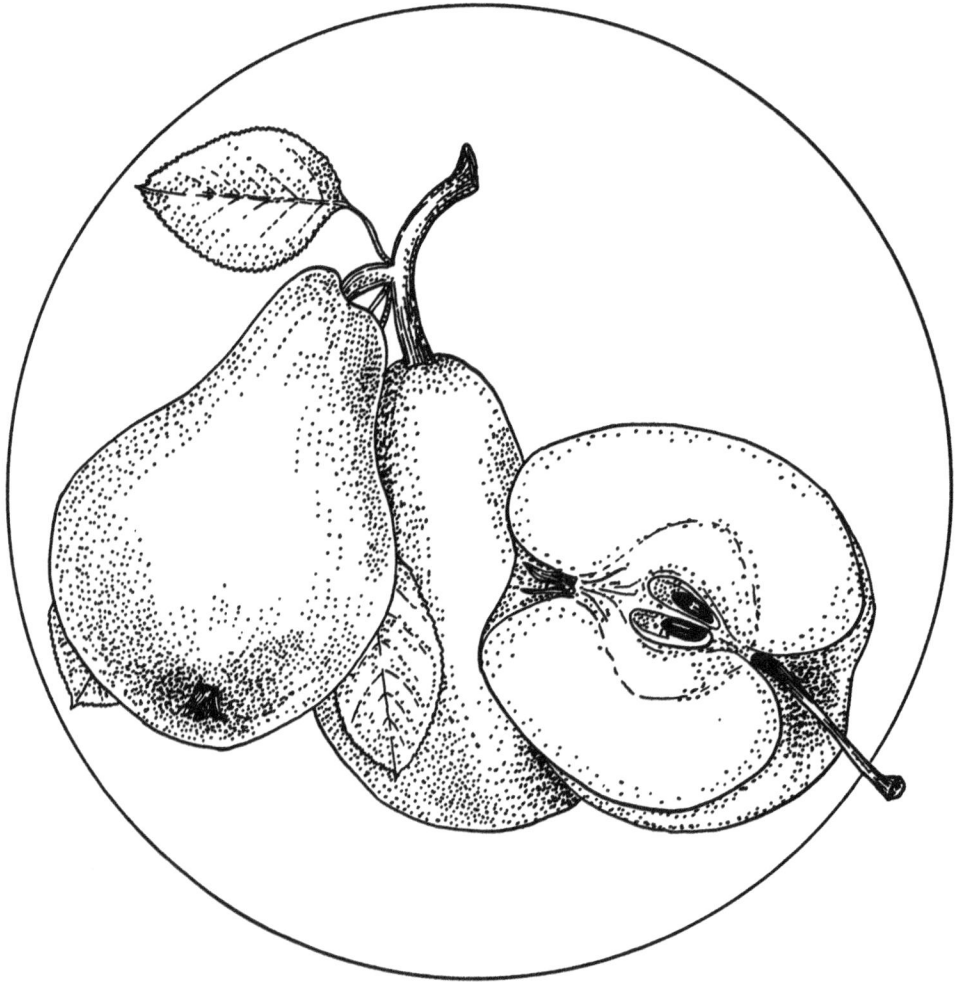

Chapter Six

Breakfast: First Things First

We hear quite a bit of debate about the importance of each meal, although breakfast is usually declared the most crucial. My own philosophy is that you should eat your most important meal at the times when you are going to be doing the most work, provided you allow enough time for some digestion in between. For children who go to school and spend the morning studying and learning, breakfast should be ample and wholesome. If they plan lots of exercise and less academic studies in the afternoon, lunch can be lighter. Adults who eat and run to work often suffer from mid-morning lag and wind up gulping coffee (mortgaged energy) to keep them going until lunch. However, if your afternoon is busy, then perhaps a medium-sized breakfast and a larger lunch are more suitable. Most people take it easy in the evening and should plan a lighter dinner. In other words, gear your meals to your levels of activity. Each child or adult must learn to listen to his or her own body signals and respond accordingly. Overeating leads to lethargy, while constant undereating can lead to weakness and an inability to concentrate. Fit the meal to suit the situation, but remember that whole foods make the best choices for any meal.

Before-school breakfasts used to cause quite in uproar in our house. While I insisted that my children eat a hearty meal, they protested that a large breakfast gave them stomachaches. Since the same big breakfast on week-ends presented no problems, I realized that the school day's inevitable tensions were the culprits. I then pushed aside all big breakfast rules and selected a lighter diet for school mornings. This lighter breakfast diet also benefits working parents who face tight time schedules. The diet involved simple, easy to prepare, whole food dishes. I saved myself time and the stomach pains soon disappeared.

The following food ideas and suggestions can be used to fit your own family's needs. The foods are divided into three basic categories: fruit, protein, and starch. Grouped together within each category are those foods that digest better together. For a light meal, choose one suggestion from one category. For heartier appetites, choose one or two suggestions from each of the three categories. These are just guidelines, so do feel free to experiment.

*F*resh Fruit Suggestions

Try to obtain unsprayed fruit. If this isn't possible, try to wash fruit in a toxin-attracting clay, available in many natural foods stores. To make a clay bath, dissolve one-half teaspoon fine clay in a large bowl of water. Dip the fruit in the solution for a couple seconds and then remove. If this sounds inconvenient, try washing all your fruits and vegetables together, right after you bring them home. If you make washing a regular part of unpacking your grocery bags, your produce will be ready to eat whenever you take it out of the refrigerator. Always be sure to eat your fruits and vegetables as soon after purchase as possible, so that they are always at their freshest (never put produce into wet plastic bags).

a. Apples, Pears, Bananas: eat whole or cut into small pieces and top with unsweetened applesauce.

b. Oranges, Grapes, Berries: make into a fruit salad, eat whole or add a handful of almonds.

c. Grapefruit, Pineapple, Grapes: halve the grapefruit and top with unsweetened grated coconut (dried or fresh). Quarter the pineapple and eat chunks along with red and green grapes.

d. Papaya, Oranges, Pineapple: slice papaya in half, reserve seeds and eat like a melon; slice orange into wedges, and pineapple into chunks.

e. Figs, Prunes, Bananas: soak figs and prunes overnight in apple juice; add ripe bananas, slice, and mix with dried fruit for compote.

f. Cherries, Plums, Peaches: combine into a fruit salad with a fruit sauce made from juice and fruit, pureed in your blender.

g. Dried Pears, Dried Apples, Dates: cook 5-10 minutes in a small amount of water or juice. Serve warm for a quick "hot" breakfast.

h. Pears, Dates (pitted), Apples: eat separately or make into a salad topped with fruit sauce.

*P*rotein-Breakfast Suggestions

Protein foods are heavier than fruit and take longer to digest. For some people, protein might be just the thing for breakfast, while for others it's too heavy. If you wish to include meat, be sure it is fresh and free from preservatives.

a. Natural cheese with acidic fruits; cottage cheese and pineapple; yogurt with berries; sour cream and peaches.

b. Nuts with fresh, acidic fruits, such as almonds and oranges, cashews and grapefruit, sunflower seeds and pineapple chunks.

c. Natural peanut butter, almond butter or cashew butter with any citrus fruit, or fruit like apples, grapes, or pears. Try spreading the nut butter on the fruit.

d. Instant protein drinks: use a natural instant protein mixed with orange juice, apple juice, or milk. Quick and nutritious, these grains can be varied by adding peanut butter, carrot, sunflower seeds, eggs, etc. (I use this idea for emergency breakfasts, when time is very short.)

e. Hard cheese (natural, not processed) with sprouts or grated into eggs for a cheesy omelette or scrambled eggs.

f. Eggs - soft-boiled, hard-boiled, poached, scrambled, any way you enjoy them.

g. Tofu: a soy bean "cheese" used by many vegetarians and cholesterol-conscious people who don't eat dairy products and need a good, complete source of protein. This bean curd can be scrambled and even made into mock egg salad.

*B*read and Cereal Ideas

Beware of too much starch in the morning; it can leave you craving nothing but starch throughout the day.

a. Hearty hot cereals such as cracked wheat, buckwheat grits, soy grits, or oatmeals with a little sweetener — maple syrup, honey, date sugar, molasses. You can use malt powder, cinnamon or nutmeg for an interesting alternative to sweetener. Also, sprouted grains are naturally sweeter.

b. Whole grain toast, whole wheat English muffins, whole wheat bagels.

c. Pancakes or waffles made with ground beans or whole grains such as whole wheat, oat, and soy. Try adding cloves, cinnamon or nutmeg to the batter for fragrant, spicy pancakes.

d. Breakfast muffins and quick breads.

Granola Ideas

a. Sprinkle on top of other hot or cold cereals.

b. Use as a topping on fruit pie, pudding, or other creamy desserts, or in making apple crisp.

c. Mix into yogurt for a smooth and crunchy combination.

d. Use as a snack in your children's lunches.

e. Layer granola with peanut butter in sandwiches.

f. Use in cookie-making.

g. Sprinkle on top of fruit salad.

h. Use on frozen bananas. (Dip ripe banana in milk or in a little honey; then roll in granola, and place in the freezer.)

i. Use in place of graham crackers for pie crust.

j. Use in casseroles where a sweet, crunchy texture is desired, or as a stuffing in acorn squash or baked apples.

Great Granola

This recipe comes in two parts: the oven ingredients are prepared first, and while they are toasting, the raw ingredients are prepared. Listed below are the oven ingredients, and on the opposite page are the raw ingredients. Enjoy!

Oven Ingredients:

5 cups flaked oats
1 cup flaked wheat
1 cup flaked rye
1 cup sorghum, honey, or barley/malt syrup
1 cup safflower oil or sunflower oil
Dash of vanilla or natural almond extract

Preparation

Preheat the oven to 350° F.

In a large bowl, mix the oats, wheat, and rye flakes. In a smaller bowl, or in a large measuring glass, mix sweetener, oil, and extract. Pour this mixture over the grains and mix thoroughly to coat the grains.

Place sweetened grains on cookie sheets (with sides) or in baking pans. Spread the grains out in one layer. Place the mix in the oven, and bake 15-30 minutes, depending on how toasted you like your grains. Every 5 minutes, turn the grains or mix with a spoon until all the grains are evenly toasted.

Raw Ingredients:

1/2 cup raw wheat germ
1/2 cup bran (unprocessed)
1 cup sunflower seeds (raw, unsalted)
1 cup chopped nuts (almonds, walnuts, cashews, etc.)
1 cup unsweetened coconut (dried or fresh)
1 cup raisins, steamed if hard to chew
1 cup chopped dried peaches, pears, or apples
Cinnamon or allspice (optional)

Preparation:

While the grains are toasting, mix all the raw ingredients—except for the cinnamon or allspice—in a large bowl or pot.

When the grains are toasted, allow them to cool for a few minutes. While they are still a little warm, break up large chunks. Sprinkle the grains with cinnamon or allspice (if you are using it), then add all the grains to the raw ingredients.

Mix well. Cool and place in jars in your refrigerator to keep fresh. Makes 15-16 cups. Use as a snack, a cereal, or in baking cookies and muffins.

*B*anana Date Muffins

Dry Ingredients:

4 cups whole wheat flour (all purpose)
1 Tbsp. baking powder (aluminum-free)
1-2 tsp. allspice

Wet Ingredients:

3-4 very ripe bananas
Dash of natural extract

1 cup of safflower oil
1/2 cup of honey or sorghum
1 cup chopped, pitted dates
Oil for muffin tins

Preparation

Oil muffin tins. Set aside. In a large bowl, combine dry ingredients. In another bowl, or in the blender, combine banana, natural extract, oil, and honey or sorghum, but do not add the dates.

Blend till liquified. Stir into dry ingredients. Mix in chopped, pitted dates so that they are evenly distributed throughout the batter. It will be easier if you toss the dates with flour before cutting them. Place the batter in paper-lined or oiled muffin tins.

Bake in 350° F. pre-heated oven for about 20 minutes or until tooth-pick comes out clean. Yield 1 1/2 to 2 dozen muffins.

Variations

a) Substitute raisins for dates; b) add 1 cup sunflower seeds or chopped walnuts with the dates; c) pour batter into well-greased loaf pans for about one regular bread size loaf.

Tropical Smoothie

Ingredients

8-10 ounces of pineapple juice or coconut-pineapple juice
1/2 ripe banana
Dash of vanilla
1-2 Tablespoons of instant protein drink (unsweetened)

Preparation

Mix juice in blender with one half ripe banana, a dash of vanilla, and instant protein drink. Blend until smooth. Serve with a little extra unsweetened coconut (dried or fresh) on top.

Feel free to add an egg, other fruit, or different kinds of unsweetened juices.

Carrot Smoothie

Ingredients

2 cups fresh, cold carrot juice
1/4 cup light cream or milk (soy, nut, or cow's)
Dash cayenne pepper

Preparation

Put blender on medium high speed for only a few seconds. Serve while frothy.

Serves 2 in regular tumblers, and more if you use cocktail glasses or juice glasses.

Snappy Apple Cider

Ingredients

4 cups fresh apple cider or juice
1/4 cup whole cinnamon sticks
1 Tablespoon whole cloves
1/8 teaspoon each, powdered cloves, ginger and allspice
1 whole vanilla bean or dash of clove extract

Preparation

Place all but 1/4 cup of cider in a saucepan. Wrap cinnamon sticks and whole cloves in a clean piece of cheesecloth and place in a saucepan. Buzz powdered spices in blender with remaining 1/4 cup of cider, and add that to pan. Add whole vanilla bean or dash of vanilla to cider and heat over low flame until warm. Remove cheesecloth mixture and vanilla bean and serve warm.

Variation

Add dash of orange or lemon extract in place of vanilla.

T.J. Cocktail

Tastes great with a side dish of crunchy peanuts or cashews.

Ingredients

2 cups tomato juice
1/2 teaspoon natural soy sauce (optional)
Juice of Vs. lemon
Dash of cayenne pepper or chili powder to taste

Preparation

Shake soy sauce, cayenne, and lemon juice in a small jar, or buzz in blender. Add chilled tomato juice. Serve with a wedge of lemon.

Sassy Sparkling Water

Ingredients

2 cups naturally sparkling water (Perrier, Calistoga) 1/4 cup frozen orange or grapefruit juice concentrate (unsweetened) 1/4 cup grapefruit juice (made from remaining concentrate)

Preparation

Buzz juice and concentrate in blender until frothy. Add to chilled Perrier and serve "on the rocks".

Variation

Add small amount of honey to blender for sweet and sassy sparkling water.

Yogurt Smoothie

Ingredients

8 oz. (unsweetened) plain, vanilla, or lemon yogurt
Fresh peach, plum, or pineapple cut into chunks
Dash maple syrup (optional)

Preparation

Whir in the blender until smooth, and serve.

Variation

Add small amount of wheat germ, lecithin, bee pollen, or bran for varying tastes.

D ried Fruit Compote

Ingredients

(Use unsulfured dried fruit)
1/2 cup dried apricots
1/2 cup dried apple rings
1/2 cup dried pears
1/2 cup prunes (pitted)
1/2 cup dried dates (pitted)
1 cinnamon stick (optional)
1 or more cups apple juice or water
Yogurt or applesauce (unsweetened)

Preparation

Soak dried fruit with cinnamon stick in water or juice for 10-15 minutes. Place soaked fruit in saucepan and cook over a low flame for 15 minutes. Remove cinnamon stick. Serve warm or cold as is, or topped with yogurt or unsweetened applesauce. This recipe can be used as a dessert, a side dish, or a breakfast dish.

H igh Fiber Cereal

Ingredients

3 cups flaked oats (non-instant)
1/2-1 cup wheat germ
1/2-1 cup unprocessed bran
1/2 cup unsweetened, dried coconut, medium or coarse
1 cup ground nuts
1/2 cup date granules, finely ground

1 cup raisins (optional)
1/2 cup banana flakes (optional)

Preparation
In a 350° oven, bake the first four ingredients on a lightly greased cookie sheet for 10 minutes. After the mixture is lightly toasted, pour into a bowl with the rest of the ingredients. Serve with milk, nut milk, or apple juice.

Easy Applesauce

Ingredients
3 pounds apples (your favorite type)
1 cinnamon stick or 1 teaspoon cinnamon powder or allspice
1/4 cup water or apple juice (approximately)

Preparation
Wash apples well; remove stems, but do not peel. Cut into small pieces and place in a large pot with a small amount of water or juice (about 1/4 cup). Add cinnamon stick if you are using one. Cook apples until they are very soft. They will be brownish in color. Remove the cinnamon stick. Put soft apples, one cup at a time, through a food mill, until all the apples have been milled. Some of the skins will remain in the mill. They can be discarded. (If you are using powdered cinnamon, add it now.) Serve warm or refrigerate until serving time. Makes about 4 1/2 cups applesauce.

Rhuberry Applesauce

Ingredients
1 cup rhubarb, cooked
3 cups thick applesauce (see "Easy Applesauce")
1/4 cup honey or barley malt (optional)
1 teaspoon vanilla
6 fresh strawberries, sliced thinly.
Unsweetened dried coconut (optional)

Preparation
Wash two bunches of rhubarb well, removing the leaves, which are poisonous. Cut the stalks into small pieces (one inch) and place in a small amount of water or apple juice. Cook, covered, over a low flame until the rhubarb is soft and the consistency of sauce. While the

rhubarb is still warm, add the honey and mix.

In a large bowl, combine the applesauce, rhubarb, and vanilla. Mix well. Slice the strawberries thinly and stir into the above mixture. Chill and serve. Makes about 4 cups. To serve, sprinkle freshly toasted coconut on top (optional). Reduce amount of sweetener gradually until only a small amount is needed. The applesauce is often sweet enough by itself, especially when apples are cooked in apple juice. Eventually you can eliminate sweetener altogether.

B aked Apples

Ingredients
6-8 Roman Beauty apples
Cinnamon, cinnamon sticks, or allspice
Apple juice
1 ripe banana
Lemon extract or lemon juice
Unsweetened coconut, toasted

Preparation
Core apples and place in a shallow baking pan. Pour small amount of cinnamon in apple centers or place 1/2 cinnamon stick in core. Pour about 1/8 cup apple juice over each apple. (Pan should have about 1" liquid, if it doesn't, add juice to pan.) Bake apples in 250° oven for about one hour or until apples are soft. Remove cinnamon sticks. Cool. Right before serving, puree banana and lemon extract in blender with apple juice to sauce consistency. Pour over apples and sprinkle unsweetened coconut on top. Reserve banana sauce until right before serving. Then pour on and enjoy. To use for breakfast, make it the night before and refrigerate. For a snack, it can be baked and served warm the same day.

M onkey Flip

Ingredients
1 cup nut milk*, or regular milk
1-2 Tablespoons unsweetened carob powder
1 banana cut into small pieces
Vanilla extract (optional)
1 Tablespoon honey (optional)

Preparation
Whirl in blender until smooth, and serve.

* Nut Milk: soak 2/3 cup nuts (almonds, cashews, hazelnuts, etc.) in one quart water overnight. Next morning, puree in blender. Strain if the nut pieces are too gritty for your taste.

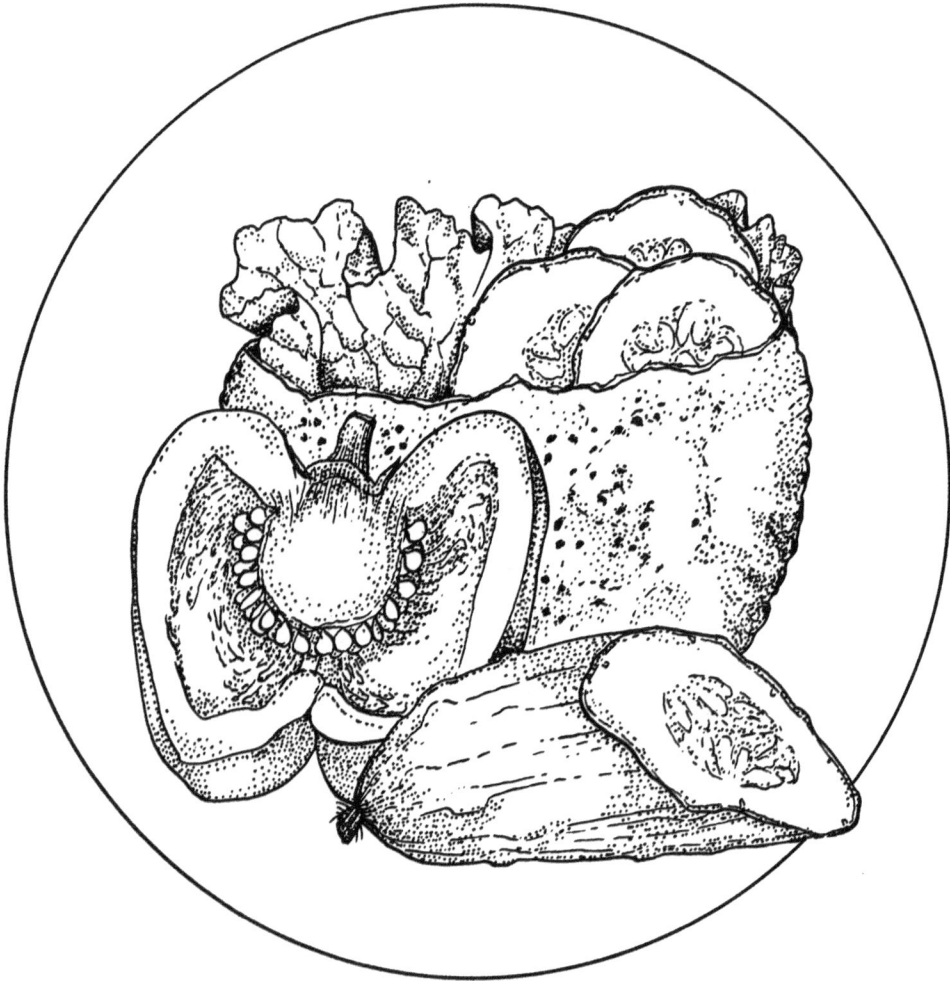

Chapter Seven

Lunch: Midday Feasts

School lunches are notorious for being over-cooked and under-nourishing. Fruits and vegetables are served from cans, the bread is white and impoverished, and desserts are generally high in refined sugar. Until your school realizes the importance of good nutrition through fresh, whole foods, the best lunch is one you make at home with your children's tastes and nutritional needs as the highest priorities.

First and foremost, sandwich bread should be whole wheat, which contains the bran and wheat germ removed from white bread. Bran provides fiber and bulk, while the germ is a good source of B vitamins. If whole wheat is a newcomer to your kitchen, introduce the idea gradually, and soon your children will be turning up their noses at white bread.

One way to interest your children in whole wheat bread is: purchase whole wheat pita (pocket) bread and make a new kind of sandwich. Pita is a flat, circular, Middle-Eastern bread with a hollow center. A piece is cut away across the top, and the cavity can be stuffed with anything. The pocket keeps the ingredients inside neatly packed. Pita sandwiches are fun to eat, fun to make, and not nearly as messy as taco shell sandwiches.

There are also many other breads to choose from: sliced rye, pumpernickel, whole wheat buns, etc. The following list includes ideas for sandwiches using the vast variety of delicious whole grain breads.

a. Natural peanut butter (no sugar, hardened oils, or preservatives added) and shredded carrots on whole wheat bread).

b. Egg salad, grated carrots, and alfalfa sprouts in pita bread.

c. Apple butter (made with a little honey or just apples), sliced ripe banana, and honey on cracked wheat bread.

d. Cream cheese (natural, not artificial) and honey on date-nut bread or Essene bread (sprouted grains formed into a round loaf). (You can substitute yogurt cheese. See recipes.)

e. Cashew butter and sliced apples on cracked wheat bread.

f. Natural, unprocessed cheese and tomatoes or sprouts on rye bread.

g. Peanut butter and alfalfa sprouts on whole wheat burger buns.

h. Chick pea spread and sprouts on whole wheat roll.

i. Banana slices, peanut butter, and fruit-sweetened jam on oatmeal bread.

j. Slivers of ripe avocado (squeeze on some lemon juice to keep green), green pepper, cucumber, and sprouts in whole wheat pita bread.

k. Peanut butter-honey-sesame spread on cracked wheat.

l. Peanut, almond, cashew, or sunflower butter and alfalfa sprouts on whole wheat crackers.

m. "Pita Hoagie" — favorite filling such as tomato, lettuce, onion, cheese, pepper, etc., topped with salad dressing and sprouts.

n. Fruit butters made only with fruit such as apple, peach, or apricot on corn bread.

o. Tahini (sesame paste), honey and wheat germ on soya-carob bread.

Soups & Such: Lunch Beyond Sandwiches

Sandwiches needn't be the only choice for your lunches. Consider using fresh fruits, celery and carrot sticks, tossed salad, or lightly sweetened yogurt to pack in a lunch. For cold days, soup in a thermos is a delicious option. In addition, many of the items listed under breakfast foods could easily be used for lunches. The following are some ideas for non-sandwich lunches that can stand alone or bolster the traditional "bread and spread" meal.

* Tomato Soup (with rice)
  Salad with cheese chunks
  Celery stalks

* Vegetable Soup
  Celery stuffed with peanut butter
  Grated carrots, chopped celery and bell pepper salad

* Cream of celery coup
  Tomato and lettuce salad with sesame seeds
  Cucumber slices

* Fruit soup
  Apple sauce
  Sunflower seeds

* Yogurt with diced fruit or vegetables
  Mixed nuts and seeds
  Warm apple juice with cinnamon

Dessert isn't really necessary for a healthy lunch. Sweet desserts can interfere with the digestion of starches and proteins. Save your children's dessert for an after-school snack. If they protest, then consider some fresh fruit, an instant protein drink, a mug of freshly squeezed juice, a mix of nuts and raisins, or yogurt. See Snack section for more suggestions.

Yogurt Cheese

Ingredients

18"x 18" cheesecloth
2 cups yogurt

Preparation

Pour yogurt into cloth lined bowl. Gather edges and tie with large rubber band or cord. Suspend from hooks with bowl positioned beneath to catch liquid. In about 6-8 hours, "cheese" should be firm enough to spread. (This depends on the brand of yogurt.) Refrigerate and use as cream cheese, adding herbs, spices, or a dash of maple syrup or natural extract for variety. Liquid (whey) in bowl can be used in baking.

F*ruits-as-a-Meal*

Ingredients

(All fruits should be ripe and, if possible, in season.)
1 pineapple
2-3 peaches
1 bunch of grapes
1/4-1/2 pound cherries
2-3 plums
1-2 papayas
1 cup strawberries
1 cup blueberries
1 cup raspberries

Preparation

Remove skin from pineapple after cutting it into quarters. Make bite-sized pieces and arrange on a flat platter with ripe cherries gently placed on top. Wash peaches and plums and place in wooden or glass bowl. Peel papayas and cut into bite-sized squares. Arrange on a flat platter with red and green grapes as a border-fruit. Wash berries and place in separate bowls or in a bowl with separate compartments, if you have one. Arrange fruit bowls and platters in a circle on your table, using color to make the setting more attractive.

Suggestions

In the middle of the table, you may wish to place a bowl of fruit-flavored yogurt sprinkled with unsweetened, toasted coconut. Or, have one or two bowls of almonds or cashews between the fruit bowls as a "crunchy" addition to the meal.

S pecial Potato Salad

Ingredients

2 pounds of new potatoes, scrubbed and cut in quarters
   (equals approximately 6 cups cooked and diced)
Fresh parsley, minced
Paprika
Sesame Seeds 1 to 1 1/2 cups alfalfa sprouts (optional)

Dressing Ingredients & Preparation

1/2 cup oil
1/4 cup lemon juice
Dash of soy sauce
1-2 garlic cloves, minced
Buzz these in blender and chill.

Preparation

To prepare hot: Place dressing in bottom of small bowl. Add cooked and diced potatoes. Sprinkle with paprika and parsley. Then toss in seeds. (Alfalfa will wilt from the heat; do not use.)

To prepare cold: After potatoes are diced, allow to cool. Then add dressing and toss. Add paprika and parsley. Toss in seeds. Right before serving, gently mix in alfalfa sprouts.

Variations

a) Substitute fresh minced dill leaves for parsley; b) use poppy or caraway seeds instead of sesame, or mix all three seeds; c) add herb of your choice — such as oregano or basil — to dressing.

E asy Eggplant Rings

Ingredients

1 medium eggplant, washed and sliced into 1/2 inch rings
1 cup tomato sauce, flavored to your taste
1 cup grated mozzarella or longhorn cheese*
Sesame seeds

Preparation

Preheat oven to 350°. Steam sliced eggplant on top of the stove for 5-7 minutes, until tender, but not mushy. Remove steamed rings gently and place on a barely oiled cookie sheet. Place approximately 1 Tablespoon sauce and 1 Tablespoon grated cheese on each slice. Bake in preheated oven for about 7 minutes, or until cheese melts and sauce is heated. Right before serving, sprinkle with sesame seeds.

Note

Serves four when part of a meal with salad and green vegetables. Can also be served over noodles, rice, or on a toasted English muffin.

Melted Cheese Pita

Ingredients

3 "loaves" whole wheat pita, cut in half, crosswise to expose
    pocket
Grated natural cheese of your choice
Slices of tomato (optional)
Alfalfa sprouts

Preparation

Stuff grated cheese and tomato into pita halves. Wrap in foil and bake in 350° oven until cheese melts. Unwrap hot foil carefully. Stuff with alfalfa sprouts and serve.

Pita Pizza with Sprouts

Ingredients

Whole wheat pita bread (6 slices to a package. Use as many
    as needed)
Tomato or marinara sauce with spices to taste
Minced garlic, onion, pepper, mushrooms
Grated skim milk mozzarella cheese*
Sesame seeds
Alfalfa sprouts

Preparation

Warm pita for about 5 minutes in 350° oven and remove. Place about 1 T. sauce on each slice, adding spices and vegetables. Top with cheese and replace pita in oven on ungreased cookie sheet, baking until cheese melts. Sprinkle each slice with seeds and top generously with sprouts.

Salad Supreme

Ingredients

1/2 head dark leaf lettuce, broken into bite-sized pieces
1/4 bead cabbage, shredded
3 radishes thinly sliced
3 or 4 cauliflowerettes, thinly sliced
1 or 2 carrots, shredded
3 green onions, sliced or chopped
1/2 cup zucchini or cucumber, sliced
1/2 cup alfalfa sprouts
1/2 cup sunflower seeds or 1/2 cup grated natural cheese
2 hard-boiled eggs, sliced (optional)

Preparation

Scrub vegetables well. Place all ingredients in a large bowl and toss lightly. Chill and serve with your favorite dressing.

Note

An easy dressing is 1 cup safflower or olive oil mixed with about 1 Tablespoon natural soy sauce (tamari) and a squirt of fresh lemon.

* Substitute tofu for cheese if you or your child is on a dairy-free diet. Tofu can be mixed in the blender or mashed with a fork and then used as a topping on the eggplant.

Middle Eastern Salad

Ingredients

Tomatoes
Peppers
Celery
Cucumbers
Onion
Sprouts
Sesame Seeds

Preparation

Mince all washed vegetables very fine (except sprouts) and place in a shallow bowl. (Juice from the minced vegetables makes a moist mixture, so a bowl is best for mixing.) Garnish with sprouts and sesame seeds. Transfer to platter and enjoy.

Chewy Carrot Salad

Salad Ingredients

4 cups scrubbed and shredded carrots
1 cup raisins, unsprayed
1 cup hulled sunflower seeds, raw or roasted without salt
1 stalk celery (scrubbed and chopped)

Dressing Ingredients

1 cup cottage cheese, ricotta cheese or tofu (soybean curd)
1 cup yogurt or buttermilk
1/2 cup mayonnaise or soft tofu
1 Tablespoon parsley flakes
1/2 teaspoon kelp (optional)
1/2 teaspoon mixed spices (basil, oregano, thyme, marjoram)
Dash curry powder

Preparation

Mix all ingredients for salad. Blend all dressing ingredients well. Gently stir dressing into salad, mixing well. Refrigerate and serve alone in a dish or topped with sprouts, if available. Serves 6-8 as side dish.

*T*abouili

Ingredients

3/4 cup bulghur (toasted cracked wheat)
1 1/4 cup boiling water
1 clove garlic, finely chopped
1/2 cup fresh thyme, finely chopped, or 2 Tablespoons dried
1 1/2 cups chopped fresh Italian parsley, or 1/2 cup dried
1 bell pepper (chopped or diced)
1 teaspoon Miso Cup*™ (optional)
1/2 teaspoon cayenne
1/2 cup olive oil (pressed)
Juice of 1/2 lemon

Preparation

Soak bulghur in 1 1/4 cups boiling water   for 1/2 hour or until all water
is absorbed.

Blend spices, oil, and lemon juice and pour over soaked grains. Mix in
chopped ingredients. Refrigerate a few hours before serving.

Variation

You can use different grains, such as kasha (toasted buckwheat), rice, or
millet, or mix several cooked grains. Also, use vegetables in season: carrots,
radish, etc.

* Powdered soybean paste from Edwards &. Sons, Union, N.J. Reconstitutes in hot, not boiling, water.

* Substitute mashed tofu if you are allergic to cheese, or cheese is not part of
your diet.

Raisin Bran Wafers

Ingredients

1 cup unprocessed bran
1 cup raisins
1 cup hot water or hot apple juice
3 1/2 cups whole wheat flour
1/4 cup soy milk or skim milk powder
1 Tablespoon baking powder (aluminum-free)
1 teaspoon allspice
1/2 cup safflower oil
1/2 cup honey or sorghum
1/2 cup apple juice

Preparation

Preheat oven to 350° F. Soak brain and raisins in hot water. Combine dry ingredients. Buzz second group of wet ingredients in blender. Add this to the raisins and bran soaking in water. Mix well. Combine this mixture with second group of ingredients. Mix well. Spoon onto lightly oiled sheets and press flat with fork. Bake about 10-15 minutes. Yield about 4 1/2 dozen small wafers.

Bean 'n' Barley Broth

Ingredients

4 quarts water
3-4 sliced carrots (1/4")
2-3 celery stalks, sliced
1 large onion
2 garlic cloves, peeled Small bunch parsley (fresh)
1 turnip or other soup "greens" such as broccoli stems, cauliflower, and cabbage cores
2 cups soaked navy beans or bean of your choice (drain and freeze after soaking to reduce cooking time)
1 1/2 cups barley (pearled)
1/4 cup Miso-Cup ™ (1 package)
Spices-thyme, dill, marjoram, and basil

Preparation

Place everything in one big pot except Miso-Cup™. Bring to a boil. Lower heat and simmer for about ½ hour. (If beans are soaked, but not frozen, this will take longer.) Then remove celery, onion, garlic, and other soup greens if you wish. (Nutrients are in water.) Blend Miso-Cup™ with a small amount of soup liquid. Stir into soup and serve.

Variation

Add 3-4 medium sized potatoes, scrubbed and diced. If beans are unavailable, substitute fresh or frozen peas at the end of the cooking period.

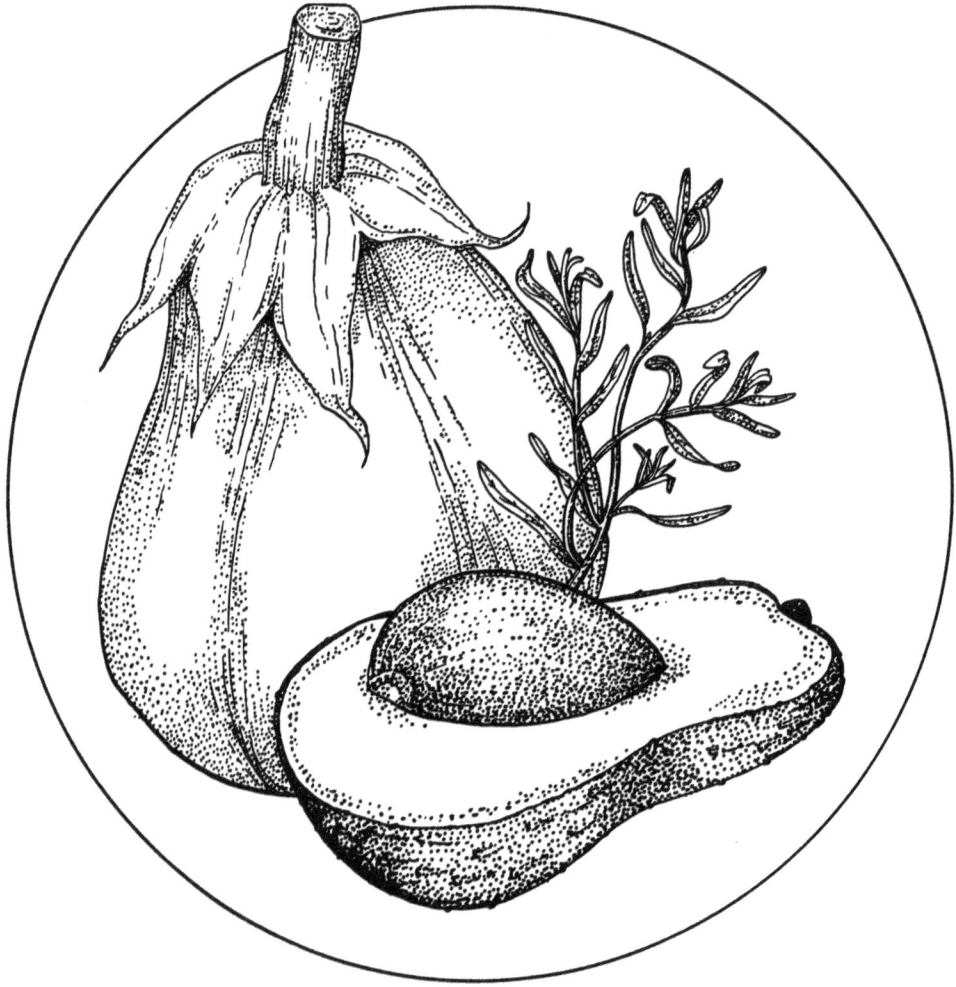

Chapter Eight

Dinner: Meatless Fare

The following dinner suggestions and recipes do not include meat. These non-meat ideas can be used as part of the meal or for the entire meal. All the suggestions are aimed at preparing simple, wholesome meals that you and your children will enjoy.

Let your children help with meal planning, including the weekly shopping. My children have learned to read all the labels on food packages and to frown at cereals, beverages, and other products that list sugar as the first ingredient. When deciding on what types of meals you'd like for the week, allow the children to participate with suggestions for different vegetables, main courses, and desserts. Children have definite likes and dislikes, but there are enough nutrients around to help keep their bodies healthy and their taste buds satisfied.

Keep in mind that the simpler the meals, the better. Since raw foods lose less nutrients in preparation than their cooked counterparts, fresh salads should be served to your family at least once a day. Teach your children how to prepare a tasty salad, to scrub the refrigerated vegetables, to peel them if skins have been sprayed with insecticides, and to cut right before serving. Try growing sprouts*, and let your children join in. Sprout-growing is a fun and educational way to add nutrients to your diet while you cut food costs.

A whole dinner can consist of a salad (either tossed or salad bar style), sprouts, steamed vegetables, and a dish made with whole grains, legumes, nuts, or cheese. If you eat meat, you can substitute that for the main protein source. If variety concerns you, don't worry. Natural foods cookbooks contain endless combinations of basic, whole ingredients. Or create your own variations from the recipes in this book.

Go slowly. If success isn't immediate, there's always tomorrow and another meal. Prepare your new foods a different way, or re-introduce them at a later time for a second try. Don't be afraid to experiment. Flops can often be recycled. If your granola is too sticky, use it in cookies; if your whole wheat bread is like a whole wheat brick, grate it into bread crumbs. Bean and grain disasters can be pureed and used for veggie burgers. Learn to be versatile and imaginative with natural foods, and you'll soon be writing your own recipe book.

Above all, don't let your new ideas about dinner throw you into a state of panic. You may not be able to manage an entire spread of new foods in one meal. Take it easy at first and introduce the different whole grains one at a time. Add fresh fruits and vegetables to your menus, but don't snatch away all of the traditional foods. Let them dwell side by side for a while; then decide which foods are the most nutritious and desirable and which ones should be eliminated altogether. You don't have to like every kind of whole food. Nature has created enough variety—and a clever cook devises even more—to satisfy everybody's tastes.

While we're on the subject of new ideas, remember that with whole foods, mealtimes need not be static: cereal for breakfast, sandwiches for lunch, and hot platters for dinner. Meals should vary according to the day's activity, the food in season, and your personal appetite. Feel free to substitute the dinner suggestions for lunch, the breakfast suggestions for snacks, and even try a salad for breakfast.

Stir Fried Rice

Ingredients

3-4 cups cooked brown rice, chilled*
1 minced garlic clove
1 cup minced vegetables (mushrooms, bell peppers, celery, carrots)
1/2 cup whole garden peas (fresh, or frozen and slightly thawed)
Spices and herbs of your choice
Sesame seeds
Oil, water or broth

Preparation

Preheat wok. Add small amount of oil, water or broth and minced vegetables. Saute and stir until softened. Then add rice and peas and stir-fry until dish is heated through, adding water if necessary to prevent sticking. Finally, sprinkle in herbs, spices, and sesame seeds. Toss gently and serve with natural soy sauce or as is.

*The proportion of rice to vegetables is at your discretion.

Stir Fried Wheat Berries

Ingredients

2-3 cups sprouted wheat kernels (berries)*
1 chopped scallion
1 grated carrot
1/4 cup diced (red) bell pepper
1/2 cup snow pea pods
Oil, water, or broth

Preparation

Preheat wok or fry pan. Add oil, water, or broth (about 1 T.) and saute scallions, carrot, pepper, and pea pods for about 1 minute. Then add sprouted wheat and stir-fry until wheat is softer, but still chewy. (If you wish to hasten this, steam wheat berries first—before putting them in wok or fry pan.) Serve immediately with a steamed green vegetable such as broccoli or zucchini.

* Proportion of vegetables to wheat berries is at your discretion.

Simple Stir Pries

Ingredients

Carrots
Bell peppers
Celery
Onion
Cabbage
Bean Sprouts (optional)
Oil, water, or broth
Almonds (optional)
Rice or Noodles

Preparation

Slice vegetables into small, uniform pieces (slivered, sliced or diced). Preheat wok or fry pan and add small amount of broth, water, or oil. Stir in vegetables in the order listed above, allowing each one to cook 2-3 minutes before adding the next. Add bean sprouts at the very end. Serve plain or with almonds, over rice or noodles.

Note
Add more liquid if necessary to prevent sticking.

S*prout Slaw*

Ingredients

1/2 white cabbage, finely grated as for coleslaw
2 to 3 carrots, scrubbed and grated
Approximately 4 ounces alfalfa sprouts Sesame seeds

Preparation

Mix all the ingredients in a bowl. Serve with your favorite coleslaw dressing or vinaigrette dressing; natural, of course.

B*ig Red Salad*

Ingredients

1/2 red cabbage, grated as for coleslaw
6 or 7 red radishes, thinly sliced
1/2 red onion, sliced (thinly) or grated
1 or 2 red beets grated

Preparation

Mix and serve on a bed of lettuce or sprouts with your favorite dressing or with a mixture of oil, lemon juice, and herbs.

S*alad Dressing*

Ingredients

1 lemon, juiced
3/4 cup safflower oil
1/4 teaspoon natural soy sauce (optional)
2 minced garlic cloves
Dash cayenne, thyme, and rosemary

Preparation

In a bottle, mix the lemon, safflower oil, soy sauce, garlic cloves, dash of cayenne, thyme, and rosemary. Shake and allow to mellow before pouring over salad.

Suggestion

Make this dressing early in the day and allow the flavors to blend for awhile. Then prepare the salad right before mealtime, pour on the dressing, and serve immediately. This salad mixture tastes great inside the pocket of pita bread, especially when the pocket is lined with leaf lettuce, and some sesame seeds are sprinkled on top.

Greg's Greek Salad

Ingredients
3-4 grated carrots, scrubbed
1-2 stalks celery, scrubbed and finely diced
1 bell pepper, finely diced

Preparation

Mix the salad ingredients in a large bowl. For a tastier salad, add a handful of alfalfa sprouts. Toss with dressing.

"Grate" Sunshine Salad

Ingredients

5 or 6 carrots, scrubbed and grated
1 or 2 yellow squash (summer), scrubbed or diced
1/2 cup yellow corn kernels, raw or lightly steamed
1/2 onion, grated or thinly sliced

Preparation

Toss and place in a bright colored bowl. Squeeze on some fresh lemon juice and garnish with fresh parsley.

Avocado Salad

Ingredients

1 ripe avocado pitted, peeled, and mashed
2 hard-boiled eggs (farm-fresh), chopped (optional)
1/2 onion, chopped finely
1/4 cup mayonnaise without preservatives
1/3 cup yogurt (plain)
Natural soy sauce, oregano, garlic powder to taste
Lettuce or sprouts

Preparation

Combine avocado, eggs, and onions in a bowl. Mix mayonnaise, yogurt, and spices in a small dish and add to ingredients in bowl. Mix well and refrigerate until serving time. Serve on a bed of lettuce or sprouts or use as a spread on whole wheat crackers. Also makes a delicious sandwich filling.

St. Patrick's Day Salad

Ingredients (any or all)

Romaine and/or leaf lettuce
Fresh spinach leaves
Alfalfa sprouts
Broccoli heads, cut small
Steamed brussel sprouts, cut in half
Green beans, raw or lightly steamed, cut into thirds
Avocado (ripe), sliced

Preparation

Wash lettuce and spinach, dry with a paper towel, and break into bite-sized pieces. Place in a large bowl with alfalfa sprouts, broccoli heads, brussel sprouts, green beans, and sliced avocado. Toss lightly and serve immediately with your favorite dressing.

"Grate" Roots

Ingredients

2 or 3 carrots, scrubbed and grated
2 or 3 beets, scrubbed and grated
1 small turnip, scrubbed and grated (optional)*
5 or 6 radishes, thinly sliced
1 garlic clove, minced
1 small onion or a few scallions, diced
Alfalfa sprouts
Safflower oil and natural soy sauce

Preparation

Toss grated root vegetables together in a bowl with alfalfa sprouts. Serve with safflower oil and natural soy sauce.

* Try Jerusalem artichoke or jicama.

Stuffed Acorn Squash

Ingredients

3 small acorn squash
Water for squash
1/2 cup brown rice
1/4 cup wild rice (optional)
1 1/2 cup water for rice
1 cup minced vegetables: peppers, onions, mushrooms
Oil or water for vegetables
Herbs to taste: parsley, oregano, thyme

Preparation

Preheat oven to 350° F. Cut squash into halves. Scoop out seeds and membrane. Place face down in pan with 1-2" water. Bake until soft (45 minutes). In the meantime, boil water. Add rinsed rice to boiling water. Bring water to a second boil. Stir, reduce heat, cover, and cook until all water is absorbed (35 minutes). While rice and squash cook, saute minced vegetables until soft.

Mix cooked rice with vegetables. Remove baked squash halves and pour remaining water off. Fill with rice mixture and replace in the oven until warm. Optional: dot each half with butter or sprinkle with sesame seeds. Serve warm. Makes 6 servings.

Tofu Quiche

Ingredients

2 Ibs. tofu, drained and pressed to remove moisture
2 cups finely chopped or torn spinach (app. 4 oz.)
1 garlic clove, minced
1/2 red bell pepper, minced
1/2 onion, grated or 2-3 scallions, chopped
Spices to taste: parsley, oregano, garlic, tamari, paprika
Oil, tomato juice, or water
Sesame seeds

Preparation

In most cases, tofu should be well drained and pressed before it is to be used. It is especially important that you drain the tofu for this recipe. Wrap the tofu in a towel, or, better yet, between two plates, and then put a heavy pot on top.

Mash drained tofu with pastry blender or potato masher. Set aside. Saute garlic, onion, and pepper in small amount of oil, tomato juice, or water. Fold into mashed tofu. Spoon into oiled pie pan or quiche pan. Bake at 350° F for about 1 hour or until top is firm and edges are browned. Sprinkle with sesame seeds and paprika and serve.

Onion-Vegetable Consomme

8 cups water or stock
3 or 4 scrubbed carrots, sliced into 1/2" rounds
6 small potatoes, scrubbed and quartered
3 or 4 celery stalks, scrubbed with leaves intact
Fresh parsley sprigs
Bay leaf
Garlic clove
Large yellow onion, sliced into thin rings

Olive oil or butter
Thyme, oregano, marjoram, or spices of your choice
1 to 2 Tablespoons natural soy sauce (tamari) or Miso-Cup™

Preparation

Add sliced carrots, quartered potatoes, and scrubbed celery to 4 cups water or stock. Bring to a boil. Add fresh parsley, bay leaf, garlic clove, and 4 more cups water or stock and simmer about one half hour. While vegetables are simmering, saute sliced onion rings in olive oil, adding spices to taste. (Add the spices to the onions first and they'll tend to stick to the onions rather than float around.)

When onions are soft and translucent, add to simmering soup. Add soy sauce to taste at this time. Allow to cook a few minutes longer, adding more spices if necessary. Serve with croutons or sesame sticks for crunchy texture.

If your diet does not permit the use of oil, butter, or salt, you can saute the onions in water from the soup, with or without a little soy sauce. Use herbs in place of soy sauce.

Cauliflower/Sweet Potato Soup

Ingredients

3-4 medium sweet potatoes
1/2 head cauliflower, broken into flowerettes
1 onion
1-2 celery stalks
1 scallion
Water
Herbs to taste
1/2 - 1 cup cooked peas, beans, or lentils (optional)

Preparation

Steam sweet potatoes in their skins. Cook, peel, and slice. Cook cauliflower and vegetables in enough water to cover. When tender, remove vegetables (discard) and strain cauliflower in colander, reserving liquid. When it cools, puree all potatoes and almost all cauliflower with a small amount of water (several batches). Return to soup pot, adding cauliflower chunks and cooking liquid to reach desired consistency.

Add garden peas or cooked beans of your choice (black-eyed peas, aduki, or lentils). Then add spices (thyme, parsley, natural soy sauce) to your taste. Simmer until all flavors blend and peas or beans are heated through.

Confetti Spaghetti

This is a variation of a recipe from Beginner's Guide to Meatless Casseroles, also published by Ross Books.

Ingredients

1 pound spinach linguini, whole wheat spaghetti, Jerusalem artichoke fettucini noodles, or corn spaghetti
1-2 cups natural grated cheese of your choice
1/2 cup mixed seeds (sesame, poppy, caraway, or your own blend)
1/4 pound margarine (soy), butter, or safflower oil (about 1 cup)
1/8-1/4 cup dehydrated onion reconstituted in a small amount of water
1 Tablespoon dehydrated garlic reconstituted as above

Preparation

Cook noodles in large pot of water with a small amount of oil. Drain cooked noodles (8-10 minutes, or according to directions on package — fresh pasta takes only about 3 minutes). Heat onions and garlic in a small amount of butter or oil in a wok or large dutch oven. Transfer noodles to the pot in which onion and garlic are sauteing. Sprinkle the mixed seeds into pot, add remaining oil or butter, and mix all ingredients gently with two large spoons or wooden forks. Then add grated cheese, toss gently again, and serve immediately. This makes 6 to 8 average servings.

Variations

Add minced vegetables, such as scallions, eggplant, green pepper, etc., to onions and garlic. Or transfer noodles to an oiled casserole, sprinkle on extra cheese, and place in the oven for a few minutes until cheese has melted.

H*oomus*

Ingredients

2 cups dry chick peas
1 jar tahini (1 Ib.)
2-3 cloves garlic
1/4 cup natural soy sauce (tamari)
1 lemon
Onion
Water from cooked beans
1-2 tsp. powdered cumin (optional)

Preparation

Soak beans overnight. Drain and place on cookie sheet. Freeze several hours. Cook frozen beans in double amount of water with onion in it or cook in a pressure cooker instead of freezing first. Blend cooked beans* and onion a little at a time, using as much water as necessary to keep blender going. Add garlic cloves, soy sauce and lemon juice to taste along with beans. If you're using cumin, add it now.

When all beans have been blended with other ingredients to a thick sauce, place in a large bowl. Add one jar of tahini and mix well, adding more tamari, garlic, or lemon juice if a stronger flavor is desired. (Add more water for thinner consistency.)

* Pureeing while still warm makes blending easier.

Place on a shallow dish, spread smoothly and sprinkle with paprika and parsley. Serve with pita strips, use as a sandwich spread, or stuff into celery.

Variations

Avocado Hoomus: mash in 1 large ripe avocado; b) Eggplant Hoomus: mash in one medium baked eggplant (no skin) and mix with cumin added to garbanzo tahini blend.

Chapter Nine

Nutritious Nibbling

Let's face it. We're in the snack generation. Everywhere we go—parties, fairs, bazaars, picnics, sports events—there are snack foods available: chips, pretzels, candy, soda, ice cream, salted nuts, popcorn, and cupcakes. Most of these popular "fun foods" have been processed with white sugar, salt, artificial colors and flavors, and chemicals to retard deterioration. And they have been linked to tooth decay, lowered body defenses to infection, allergic reactions, and behavioral problems.

Kicking the junk food habit won't be easy. If your family rejects a natural snack you want to substitute for the usual chips and pretzels, don't give up. Their palates have been adulterated. Sugar is addictive, satisfies the need for quick energy, and dominates the taste of sweetened snacks, making unsweetened treats initially less appealing. Salt has a similar effect, and palates that have been "perverted" by these two culprits take some time to be reeducated.

Start by sharing your plans with your children, your spouse, and any other relative who is in the habit of giving out snack foods. Tell them about your concerns—how you want to eliminate "foodless" snack foods and replace them with real food snacks. If your children are old enough to read, give them some easy books on food and nutrition (see resource list of children's food books). Once you make them an active part of your plan, you might find a more positive response to your changes.

Then, make a list of the times and places where snack foods are most often served: birthday parties, after-school trips, picnics, circuses, school parties, etc. Either choose a specific snack time for serving only natural food snacks or slowly introduce one or two items at each occasion. Gradually add one more natural snack until the entire menu finally contains ingredients that are good tasting as well as good for you. In the beginning you may have to fudge—you may first serve natural potato chips made without preservatives, and without lower grade oils, to replace the traditional counterpart. An intermediate step or two eases the transition to healthy snacking. However, potato chips, natural or not, are still fried and often salted potatoes, and sooner or later need to be edged out of your snacking habits. Fortunately, there are plenty of delicious, nutritious alternatives, such as nuts, seeds, and fruit.

The following suggestions are divided into two groups: the first group is for the slower, sneakier, "fudge" method; the second group is to be used once you've made the transition. Whether you incorporate these ideas and recipes on a random basis or with a deliberate determination to make each snack session more wholesome, you will soon feel a real sense of achievement as your children ask for fruit juice, whole grain cookies, or your salt-free nut and raisin mixture. Enlist you children's help in preparing nutritious munchies and teach them to make their own. They can learn right along with you to use wholesome ingredients for scrumptious snacks.

Suggestions for Gradual Natural Snack "Fudging"

a. Mix your regular peanut butter with a brand made without additives, sugar, or extenders.

b. Mix traditional salted nuts and seeds with unsalted nuts and seeds, using less and less of the salted as you become accustomed to their natural taste.

c. Make popcorn from unsprayed kernels for an afternoon or evening snack.

d. Substitute unsalted whole wheat pretzels for regular pretzels.

e. Use granola for snacking, either plain, or as a cereal. Careful—if the first ingredient is sugar, even brown sugar, pick a less sweet brand or make your own, with your kids' help.

f. Place fresh or dried fruit (unsulfured) in a bowl on the table, next to their traditional snacks during the transitional stage. Eventually your family will grow to consider fresh fruit a perfect snack.

g. Slowly replace cookies, sugary cakes, and donuts made of white flour and white sugar with baked goods made from whole grains and natural sweeteners. Buy them natural or bake them. Baking is a good rainy day project for your children. You might even suggest a natural bake-in for a scout group, boys and girls.

h. Make hot cocoa with half chocolate and half carob powder (unsweetened). Chocolate not only contains caffeine but sometimes causes allergic reactions in allergy-prone children. Moreover, most commercial chocolate has great amounts of sugar, not to mention chemical flavorings. Carob is a natural chocolate-like ingredient that comes from carob pods. It has none of the harmful ingredients found in chocolate.

Naturally Good Snack Ideas

a. Fresh carrot sticks or celery sticks stuffed with peanut, almond or sunflower butter, yogurt or cream cheese and sprinkled with sprouts.

b. Chocolate-like treats made with unsweetened carob powder. Substitute natural carob for chocolate in recipes.

c. Whole grain crackers with natural spreads—unprocessed cheese, jams, nut butters, or fruit butters.

d. Smoothies (blender drinks) made from natural ingredients.

e. Unsweetened apple sauce or baked apples.

f. Fresh fruit on skewers—fruit kabobs (good for parties) .

g. Date treats made from unsulfured dates and stuffed with natural cheese or nuts.

h. Pink Pudding.

i. Frozen bananas on a stick.

j. Homemade cookies and cakes.

k. Cooked, cold sweet potatoes (similar to a banana in consistency).

l. Fresh fruit salad.

If you have very little time to prepare some of these snacks, visit a natural foods store and check out their snack section. Keep an eye out for added sugar, whether it be honey or tubinado sugar. Avoid snacks made with salt or fried in oil.

Snacks for Special Occasions

For more specific snack times, here are a few menus that use some of the previous suggestions:

Meal Style Birthday Party
Carrot and celery sticks
Homemade whole wheat pizza
Freshly squeezed orange juice
Yopsicles

Snack Style Birthday Party
Nuts, seeds and raisin mixture
Fruit punch
Frozen bananas or banana freeze ice cream
Yoatmeal Cookies or Granola-Applesauce cookies
Popcorn balls using organic popcorn, or a natural corn or rice puff cereal, and barley corn-male

Teen Party
Sunburst Dip with
Vegetables
Smoothies or Sparkling Water
Peanuts in the shell Homemade soup in mugs
Caroballs

Travel Food
Rice cakes spread with non-sugared jams
Whole wheat bread or rolls, spread with natural peanut,
   almond, or cashew butter and topped with alfalfa sprouts.
Unsulfured dried fruits
Caroballs
Granola bars (without sugar)
Fresh fruit in season
Carrot and/or celery sticks or Jerusalem Artichoke slices
Travel munchies
Whole wheat pretzels
Dried banana chips (unsweetened)

Picnic Menu
Fresh tossed salad using vegetables in season with natural dressing added at time of eating
Potato salad or macaroni salad with natural mayonnaise
Whole wheat Pita bread sandwiches with various fillings; egg salad, sprouts, and grated carrots; or grated cheese, tomato, and sprouts.

Learning new eating habits isn't always easy, especially when your children are faced with peer pressure at school or on the playground. Persistance pays off, so stick to your goals, and you'll soon be blessed with children who respect the importance of real food. If they slip occasionally, don't give up or become angry. They need to grow accustomed to the change and will soon know what makes them feel better. The more you move away from highly salted snacks and heavily sugared desserts, the more your family will appreciate the taste of fresh fruit, wholesome homemade desserts, and real juices. Then, when you do treat yourselves to snack food, it will be a real treat because it won't be an everyday habit. Snacking may be part of our busy modern lifestyle, but there's no reason it can't be a natural and healthy part of our diet.

No-Cook Caroballs

Dry Ingredients
1 cup carob
1 cup milk powder (non-instant) or soy milk powder

Wet Ingredients
1 cup natural liquid sweetener (sorghum, barley-malt, syrup, or honey)
2 cups natural peanut butter
Dash natural extract (almond, lemon, or vanilla)
1/4 - 1/2 cup safflower oil
Dried, unsweetened coconut, and/or toasted sesame seeds

Preparation

In a large bowl, mix carob and milk powder. In a smaller bowl, mix sweetener, peanut butter, vanilla, and va cup oil. Add both mixtures together. Mix well. If too dry to form into balls, add a little more oil. The consistency should be like fudge, but not too wet.

Shape into balls and roll in coconut or sesame seeds. Yields about 30 golfball-sized caroballs.

Variations

a) Add nuts, seeds, raisins, or granola to the basic recipe, b) Use different extracts, such as orange or butterscotch. Add wheat germ or bran, adding water if necessary to keep fudge-like consistency, c) Substitute protein powder or nutritional yeast for milk powder and substitute almond butter for peanut butter, d) Use molasses in place of honey, sorghum, or barley corn-malt. Roll in granola, sunflower meal, or date powder.

Granola Applesauce Cookies

Dry Ingredients

2 cups whole wheat flour or mixed flours. For example, one
    cup whole wheat, 1/2 cup oat, and 1/2 cup soy flour
1/4 cup milk powder, soy milk powder, or protein powder
1 teaspoon cinnamon or allspice
2 cups granola

Wet Ingredients

1 cup unsweetened applesauce
1/2 ripe banana
1 teaspoon pure vanilla extract
1/2 cup safflower oil
1/2 cup unsweetened apple juice

Preparation

Mix dry ingredients in large bowl. Blend wet ingredients in a blender. Add wet ingredients mixture to dry ingredients mixture and mix well. Spoon onto lightly greased cookie sheets and press down with a wet fork. Bake in a preheated 350° oven about 15 minutes. Cool and serve. Store in the refrigerator. Yields: 4 1/2 dozen small cookies.

Applicious Cookies

Dry Ingredients

1 cup oat flour
1 cup whole wheat flour
2 teaspoons allspice
1 cup hulled sunflower seeds

Wet Ingredients

1 cup unsprayed raisins soaked in 1/3 to 1/2 cup apple juice

1/2 cup unsweetened apple butter
1 grated apple
1 teaspoon pure extract (almond, vanilla)
1/4 cup safflower oil
1/2 cup honey, sorghum, or barley-malt syrup

Preparation

Preheat oven to 350°. Combine wet ingredients in large bowl and dry ingredients in another bowl. Add dry mixture to wet mixture and mix well. Drop by spoonfuls onto lightly greased cookie sheets. Bake for 12-15 minutes. Yields approximately 3 dozen cookies.

Yoatmeal Cookies

Ingredients

2 cups flaked oats, lightly toasted
1 cup dried, unsweetened coconut
1 ripe banana, peeled and mashed
1/4 cup plain yogurt
Dash of natural extract (lemon, orange, mint, vanilla or almond)
1/2 cup honey or barley/malt syrup or maple syrup
1/2 cup powdered milk or protein powder
1/2 cup carob powder (unsweetened)
Allspice to taste
Additional (toasted) coconut

Preparation

Toast oats in a low oven (300° F.) for about 10 minutes. You may also toast the coconut. If you do, watch the temperature; coconut burns easily.

While oats are in the oven, mix banana, yogurt, extract, and sweetener in a large bowl, blending well. Then stir in the milk, carob powder, and allspice.

Remove toasted oats from oven and stir into wet mixture, adding in raw coconut; or, if toasted, add coconut automatically with oats from the same bake pan.

When ingredients are well mixed, form balls with your hands, and roll in additional coconut. Flatten onto a cookie sheet or platter and refrigerate. To hasten the hardening process, you may freeze them for about one hour.

These cookies will never be as hard as a baked cookie, but the freezing will help to firm them. Yields approximately 3 dozen cookies.

Variation
Feel free to add chopped nuts, steamed raisins, or sunflower seeds for more crunch.

Note
The milk powder and carob powder plus water make a good icing.

Strawberry Stix or Fruit Kabobs

Ingredients

Pineapple chunks (fresh if possible)
Fresh strawberries, washed
Apples
Pears and/or papayas
Maple syrup
Unsweetened coconut
4 inch or 6 inch bamboo skewers

Preparation

Wash and cut fruit into bite-sized pieces. Sprinkle on some lemon juice as you work, so the fruit does not turn brown.

When the fruit is cut, place in a shallow bowl of maple syrup, a few pieces at a time. Using a slotted spoon, place fruit that has been well-coated with syrup into a bowl of fresh, unsweetened coconut.

Gently toss the fruit until it is well-covered with coconut. Then take a bamboo skewer and spear the pieces of fruit on the skewer: strawberry, pineapple chunk, strawberry, pear piece, strawberry, apple piece, strawberry, etc.

Continue until the skewer is filled, with a little space at the unpointed end for handling. Once the skewers are filled, place ka-bobs in the refrigerator.

Note

If you have any leftover fruit, syrup, or coconut, mix them all together and add to unsweetened yogurt to use as a dessert or snack for your family. Also, as you wean your family from sweets, you can assemble the ka-bobs plain, using just fresh fruit. Or if you wish to sweeten it naturally, soak some dried fruit in apple juice and alternate fresh fruit with plump, dried pieces.

Granola Brownie Bars

Dry Ingredients

3 cups whole wheat flour
1 cup unsweetened carob powder
1-2 teaspoons allspice

Wet Ingredients

1 1/2 cups water or juice (unsweetened)
1 cup natural peanut butter
1 cup sorghum, honey, or barley-malt syrup
Oil for baking pan

Both layers

5 cups naturally sweetened granola

Preparation

Thoroughly oil (liquid lecithin works well here) a lasagna-type baking pan (11" x 16") or a large baking pan with 2" high sides. Set aside. Set oven to 350° F. Mix dry ingredients in large bowl. Mix wet ingredients in another bowl. Stir wet ingredients into dry in a third bowl, to a thick batter-like consistency.
Sprinkle 3 cups granola on bottom of oiled pan. Pour batter over granola, carefully spreading with spatula to cover granola. Sprinkle remaining 2 cups

granola over batter. Cover with foil. Bake for V4 hour or until toothpick comes out clean. Remove foil and allow pan to cool. When cool, cut into bars 1" x 2" or any small size you wish. Store in cookie jar or refrigerator in warm weather.

Cooked Carob Icing

Ingredients

1 cup honey or sorghum
1 stick butter or (soy) margarine
Carob (approximately 1/2 cup)
Unsweetened coconut (dried or fresh)

Preparation

Melt honey and butter in a double boiler. Add enough carob to thicken the mixture to a spreadable consistency. Cool and ice three layer cake or muffins, spreading thinly, as this is quite sweet. You may spread icing between the layers or use jam. Sprinkle cake or muffins with coconut for eye appeal.

Yopsicles

Ingredients

2 fresh peaches, cut into small chunks
One cup plain or (unsweetened) vanilla yogurt
Dash of maple syrup
Unsweetened dried coconut

Preparation

Puree cut peaches, yogurt, and syrup (more or less to taste) in blender. Stir in coconut (just enough to add some crunch) and pour into popsicle molds or paper cups. Freeze until firm. (Sticks can be inserted in paper cup molds when yogurt mixture is partially frozen.)

Variations

Use other fleshy fruits in season, such as nectarines or apricots. Substitute ground nuts for coconut. Add natural extracts, such as lemon, orange, or butterscotch.

Tofruit Dip or Pudding

Ingredients

1/2 pound firm tofu, drained (or ricotta cheese)
2-3 oz. apple juice or strawberry-apple juice
8 oz. lemon or strawberry yogurt. Use unsweetened, with frozen or fresh strawberries.
Maple syrup to taste

Preparation

Blend tofu with juice. Remove and stir in yogurt by hand, adding maple syrup to taste. Use as a fruit dip or pudding. For pudding, you may wish to use less juice, depending on how thick you like it.

Pink Pudding

Ingredients

1/2 cup unsweetened grape juice or cranberry juice
1 apple, cut into small pieces (peel if sprayed)
1 cup fresh or fresh frozen whole cranberries
16 oz. plain unsweetened yogurt, or substitute vanilla or lemon
Unsweetened coconut (dried or fresh), chopped walnuts, or granola

Preparation

Place juice in blender. Add apples and cranberries and puree with juice. Remove mixture from blender and place in a bowl. Stir in yogurt to make a smooth mixture. Place in serving dishes. Right before serving, sprinkle on coconut, nuts, or granola. Yields about 4 cups.

Halvah

Ingredients

Tahini (sesame paste)
Honey
Ground almonds
Dried, unsweetened coconut

Preparation

Cream equal amounts of honey and tahini. Add ground almond until a thick mixture results. Press mixture into a bar (or into balls), rol in coconut, wrap in the refrigerator, and allow to harden. Slice a needed. Feel free to use different nuts. Eventually reduce honey anc incorporate all tahini.

* A middle eastern food (candy), generally made with lots of sugar. This is a natura counterpart, so it does not taste or look exactly like the real thing.

Cashewberry Crush

Ingredients

2 cups sliced fresh strawberries
2 cups ground, unsalted cashews
1 cup unsweetened juice (apple, grape, or apple/strawberry)
Dash maple syrup (optional)
Unsweetened coconut (dried or fresh)

Preparation

Place berries, cashews, and juice in blender or processor and blend to a thick puree. Place in serving dishes, sprinkle on some coconut, and top each dish with a fresh berry. Yields about 4 cups.

Variation

Add a little more juice for a thinner consistency and use as a topping for fruit salad.

Bananas-on-a-Stick 1

Ingredients

3 ripe, but firm, bananas
Maple syrup
Dried coconut, unsweetened
Granola, homemade if possible
Popsicle sticks

Preparation

Cut bananas into thirds or halves. (Small bananas into halves; large, into thirds). Place popsicle stick in the flat end of banana. Roll banana pieces in small amount of maple syrup and then in coconut and/or granola. Place bananas on a tray lined with wax paper and put in freezer. Serve when firm.

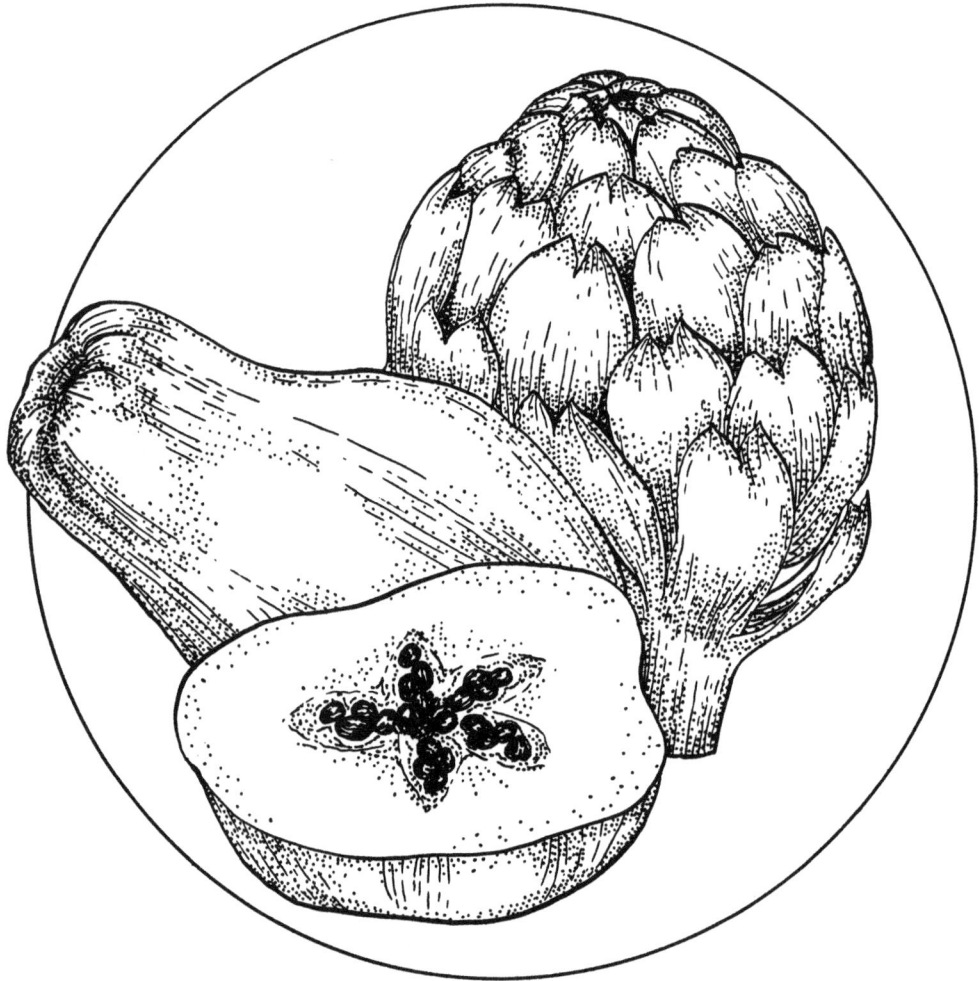

Chapter Ten

Babies: Whole New Lives

Having a baby is one of life's most joyous experiences. Raising a truly healthy child increases that joy immeasurably. This chapter is designated to help you start your baby off to a happy, natural childhood.

As soon as you and your spouse decide to have a child, both of you should adopt a healthy pre-conception diet. Begin by eliminating caffeinated drinks (coffee, tea, and colas), alcoholic beverages, and smoking. These "social substances" tend to be used compulsively, and are in general more detrimental than recreational. They are definitely non-nutritional. Caffeine, alcohol, and tobacco (and possibly even marijuana) have been linked with male sterility, delivery problems, and abnormal fetal development, not to mention cancer.

Avoid all prescriptive and non-prescriptive drugs, even aspirin. If you are on special medication and are not sure you can give it up cold turkey, ask your doctor about slow withdrawal. Always ask if any drug you are taking could harm a growing fetus—and get more than one opinion. Ideally, you and your spouse should be in excellent health before you even decide on a family. In the case of an inherited or congenital problem, you might consider seeking a nutritionally-oriented doctor.* He/she can suggest alternative medications that have as few side effects as possible. Whatever a pregnant woman eats passes into the placenta, and you want only wholesome nutrients to reach your baby.

While heredity and other important factors cannot be dismissed, a healthy diet is a prerequisite for a healthy baby. Establish good habits before your pregnancy, and your baby will enter an environment in which conscious nutrition and health play an important part in everyday life.

Once pregnant, a mother-in-waiting must be especially careful to continue her intake of healthy foods. During your pregnancy, adopt a diet consisting of high quality protein, yellow and green leafy vegetables, fresh fruits and fruit juices, sprouts and raw vegetable salads, whole grains, and nuts. These foods should be served in proportions suited to the individual's needs.

Follow the same common sense eating habits started before conception. Pregnant women should not not go on crash diets. Increase portions according to the changing needs of your body. A pregnant mother should satisfy her appetite without becoming unnecessarily overweight for her condition. One hint is to eat lots of raw foods. Many nutrients are destroyed in cooking, while raw foods not only have their vitamins and minerals intact, but they possess precious enzymes needed for digestion. Eating unadulterated, fresh foods makes good sense in more ways than you can count, especially when you have two healthy bodies to feed.

A nutritious diet before and during pregnancy is of primary importance to producing a healthy baby. Once the baby is born, concern usually shifts to the newborn's diet, but don't forget that a new mother's diet is still very important to her baby's well-being. Breastmilk from a healthy mother is the only food suitable for a newborn child. If mother's diet consists of raw or lightly cooked, wholesome dishes made from simple, pure foods, she will feel stronger sooner and provide quality breastmilk for her infant.

The subject of introducing solid foods has provoked much controversy. Most enlightened doctors recommend postponing cereals for several months. Strained fruits and vegetables are easier to digest, and are recommended for infants as young as 3-6 months or as old as 1-2 years.* When introducing any new food, it should be the only solid ingested for several days to avoid and isolate any allergic reaction.

The longer the mother waits to introduce each new food, the less chance there is of this kind of an allergic reaction. As the baby's digestive system matures, s/he is better able to handle complex foods. It's best not to introduce any solids until your baby has teeth. The ability to handle solids does vary from baby to baby, so the parents have to be the final judge. Vegetables make an excellent start; sweet fruits may whet an undesirable appetite for sweets.

Start with soft fruits when giving solids to your baby, like very ripe, mashed banana. Two or three types of vegetables and fruits can be used as whole meals, once Baby has learned to tolerate each one. Do not mix fruits and vegetables at the same meal, even if they have not caused any difficulties by themselves. Since each food category requires different kinds of digestive enzymes, mixing fruits and vegetables can impede digestion. We parents are used to the taste of flavored and spiced food, but babies enjoy food in its natural state: unsalted, unspiced, and certainly not overcooked.

---

* People should see nutritionally oriented doctors on a regular basis, even if there aren't any obvious inherited problems. These doctors are sometimes hard to find, though their numbers are increasing. For more information, Alacer Corp. puts out a booklet entitled Nutrition Minded: Doctors in the U.S. and Canada (Alacer Corp., Buena Park, CA 90622, $1.00). Also see the Association for Holistic Health's The National Directory of Holistic Health Progress (San Diego, CA: Association of Holistic Health 1982, $7.95).

Commercial baby foods have no place in your baby's wholesome diet, except, perhaps, in rare cases—when you are travelling long distances by public transportation, for example. Parents can easily puree fresh fruit in a food grinder or steam and mash vegetables. Even though many baby foods now exclude salt, sugar and starch, they still can't compare with the fresh taste, good quality, and low price of foods made from scratch.

Complex starches, such as cooked whole grains and potatoes should not be fed to the baby until s/he has a full set of teeth (or at least grinding molars), between one and two years. Meat is even more difficult to digest. If cereals and complex starches are hard to handle, imagine the difficulty a baby has with fatty, fibrous, heavy meats, pureed or not. I recommend an even longer postponement of meat than of other foods, as much as eight years, if you intend to introduce it at all.

Breastmilk fills all the baby's protein needs. If breastfed until two, the baby also has an ample supply of the calcium necessary for proper formation of teeth. If the mother breastfeeds for at least two years, then milk need not even be added to the baby's diet. If, however, you find breastmilk inadequate, then goat's, soy, or nut milk are all easier for Baby to digest than cow's milk.

Certainly your new child will one day try junk foods. Hopefully, good food habits started from day one will help him or her to recognize them as the junk they are. By the time your own children become parents, their offspring will have twice as healthy a start in life as you did. Don't wait until your children begin planning their own family to give prenatal nutritional advice. Start now. Ensure that your grandchildren enjoy the benefits of a truly healthy life. We owe at least that much to our posterity.

A Word About Breastfeeding

Breastmilk is, of course, the ideal food for infants. In fact, it is the only food the baby needs for at least six months, providing the mother has been on a healthy diet. Babies digest breastmilk more easily than formula—especially formula made from cow's milk (each species' milk is specifically geared to the growth needs of its own offspring). Breastfed babies have fewer skin problems, are less likely to suffer from allergies or anemia, and breastmilk provides them with a natural immunity to infections. (For more information on the many advantages of breastfeeding, see Dr. Paavo Airola's Everywoman's Book.) With at least a dozen excellent reasons for breastfeeding, continued formula feeding is hard to understand. Even a working mother can express her milk and have

---

* I started my last child on whole vegetables and fruits at 9 months.

a sitter feed it to the baby at a later hour.

All newborns need and deserve to be breastfed, even if only for a couple of months, but, for a variety of reasons, many Americans simply cannot do this. If the use of formula becomes necessary as a supplement to breastmilk, parents have the responsibility to provide a superior product. Years ago, mothers made their own formulas, but now formula companies provide that service. I suggest a thorough investigation of any formula company's product before your baby is born. You may wish to consult the local hospitals to see what they use, or ask different pediatricians what they recommend. A new, all-natural infant formula called NaturLac is now available, but it does contain whole cow's milk, which may not be easily digestible for infants. This formula is free of the preservatives, chemicals, and salt NaturLac claims other formulas contain. You may also investigate the possibility of goat's milk as an alternative to cow's milk. Some nutritionists claim goat's milk is better than cow's because the organs of a goat are similar to those of an adult human, making the milk composition for goat kids more digestible for human babies.

When breastfeeding is not the chosen method for the future parents, the responsibility of finding a safe and wholesome alternative to mother's milk can be overwhelming, especially if later the infant is found to be allergic to the formula (as was the case with my first child). The problem of proper formula feeding is of crucial importance, since a liquid diet is all a young baby can handle. It's better to try breastfeeding first and if this doesn't "feel" right,* mother can always switch over to formula, but usually not vice versa.

Simple Foods for Baby

Vegetables

Consider avoiding foods high in oxalic acid, such as spinach, sorrel, and rhubarb leaves. According to Peter Wengate's Medical Encyclopedia, oxalic acid corrodes the lining of the mouth and stomach and interferes with nerve and muscle fibre function by neutralizing the calcium in body fluids. The latter is necessary for nerve conduction and muscle contractions (p. 324). Feeding these foods to infants less than three months can be especially hazardous (solid foods should not start for at least 6 months anyway). If, for some reason, you do start your children on solids this early, begin with fruits or other vegetables.

Use fresh, unsprayed vegetables, in season whenever possible. Steam or cook in a very small amount of pure water. Mash with fork or process in a baby food grinder until your baby can eat whole, cooked pieces with fingers or utensils. Do not serve the vegetables hot. Room temperature is easier for the body to handle, both in the hand and in the digestive track.

As soon as possible, let an older baby with many teeth eat vegetables as a finger food in a raw or lightly steamed form. Fewer nutrients are lost by eating vegetables and fruits that have been cooked as little as possible. Following are some finger food suggestions:

Wash *Asparagus* well; discard the hard white stalks, steam, and serve the tips to Baby. Eat the green stalks yourself, until Baby can chew them thoroughly.

Wash and steam *Artichokes*; cut up the hearts for Baby. Puree or serve in small, soft pieces. When your baby has more teeth, let him/her use them to scrape the inside of the leaves.

Scrub, slice, steam, and serve *Beets* pureed, or in small pieces as finger foods, when your baby can chew.

Steam and serve *Broccoli* tops, pureed at first and later in small pieces as finger food. Leftover stalks can be peeled, sliced, and steamed in mixed dishes for the rest of the family until Baby's teeth can handle somewhat tougher foods.

Steam or cook Brussel Sprouts until soft; puree or serve in pieces as teeth come in.

Steam or cook *Carrots* in small amounts of water, then puree and serve. When Baby's teeth come in, cut carrots into slices, steam, and serve as finger food vegetables. A firm carrot also makes a good teething item, but be careful; Baby could choke on small pieces.

Postpone raw *Celery* until your baby has enough teeth for grinding and chewing. You can, perhaps, stuff raw celery with a moist nut butter which won't catch in the throat. This is for the older infant or toddler.

Postpone *Corn*, a vegetable which is hard to digest, until baby's second year. Then s/he may even be able to eat it right off the cob after it has been cooked. Avoid popcorn.

---

* Consider attending La Leche League meetings. These are support groups of mothers who breastfeed or are considering breastfeeding. Encouragement and help in difficult situations

For *Cucumber*, slice and peel (if waxed). It makes a good finger food when Baby can chew. Cold cucumber may soothe sore gums. It can also be pureed in blender and served as "cuke soup."

Serve small, crisp *Lettuce* leaves as a finger food or as a grated, raw vegetable dish. Do not cook.

Lightly steamed or raw, *Mung Bean Sprouts* are quite crunchy and can be eaten alone or mixed with other vegetables. Alfalfa sprouts tend to gag in an infant's mouth; wait until Baby can chew well. Sprouts are a good source of nutrients when raw, so hold off until you can serve them uncooked or lightly steamed.

Bake or mash sweet *Potatoes*, a favorite for many babies. White potatoes are drier so you may want to postpone them until the baby's salivary glands are better developed.

Steam and mash shelled *Peas* until Baby has enough teeth to chew raw, whole garden peas. Then, use as finger food, either raw or lightly steamed.

Steam red *Bell Peppers* (sweet) or use raw, as teeth allow.

Peel, steam, and mash *Summer Squash* (yellow and zucchini) until Baby can eat them raw or in steamed slices.

Postpone serving *Tomatoes* until your baby's second year, and then not with starchy vegetables. Tomatoes often cause allergic reactions, such as diaper rash. Actually fruits, but usually grouped with vegetables, tomatoes are best served with more "fruity" vegetables like cucumbers and peppers.

Note: Remember that eggs, flesh foods, and cheese are concentrated protein and should be introduced sparingly, if at all.

*F*ruits

Fruits are often the first food given to a baby, especially fruit juices. If you decide to feed fruit first, make sure the ones you choose are fresh and very ripe. Fruit canned in syrup is unnecessary and may lead to the desire for sweets. Mashing a ripe banana or papaya instead is both simple and wholesome.

---

make breastfeeding more attractive to the hesitant mother. (Address in Resource Section under Newsletters)

Puree raw peeled Apples in blender for homemade applesauce. Don't use raw chunks until chewing teeth are developed.

Mash well-ripened Avocado; eventually your baby will be able to eat small, raw pieces. When very ripe, avocados can almost be gummed.

Mashed ripe Banana is supposed to taste like mother's milk and is often given as the first food. Later, whole bananas are a perfect snack, easy to carry in a purse or a car. Frozen, bananas can be used to sooth gums.

Remove the pits from fresh Cherries and serve them in a ground form until your baby is old enough to handle the whole fruit.

Serve Citrus Fruits (oranges, grapefruits, tangerines, tangeloes) pureed at first, then eventually in sections as a finger food.

Soak, and then chop or puree Dried Fruits. These are high in natural sugar, so brush teeth after eating.

You may have to peel Grapes before they can be eaten by an infant. Eventually seedless grapes can be served whole. Raisins (dried grapes) are very concentrated and should be served only occasionally, soaked in water and then followed by toothbrushing.

Kiwi Fruit is a fuzzy little tropical fruit. Soft and sweet, it can be spooned into baby's mouth when the fruit is ripe, and Baby can chew. (The peel is not eaten.)

Ripe, soft Melons can be easily mashed and eventually eaten in chunks as finger food. Melon is digested best when eaten alone.

Peel, mash, or puree Papaya at first, then serve this soft sweet fruit in pieces as finger food.

Ripe Pears are buttery soft and can be easily mashed. Eventually slice them and serve in pieces.

Sweet, ripe Pineapples are hard to find. Find a good source or avoid this fruit. Postpone serving pineapples until Baby's mouth is full of teeth, since they are harder to chew than the fleshy fruits. Serve in small chunks.

Fresh, ripe Plums can be pitted, mashed, or pureed. Later, Baby can eat them whole.

Cook Rhubarb in apple juice (to avoid tartness), puree, and serve. Use sparingly. Remember, the leaves are poisonous.

Grains

Grains are hardest to handle and should not be introduced as early as fruits and vegetables. If you postpone grains until Baby's grinding teeth are in, they can be cooked and served just as you would for the rest of the family. There is no need to buy highly processed baby cereals if you wait until Baby is ready to eat whole grains. Those who wish to start grains earlier should consult natural baby food cookbooks. Grains go best with green and yellow vegetables, raw or steamed. When sprouted, they increase in nutrients, cook in less time, and are sweeter-tasting.

Eggs

Eggs are one of the foods high on the list of allergies. Postpone until second year, if possible, to avoid allergies. Eggs are considered a complete protein, but someone allergic to eggs does not benefit from the nutrients.

Sample Menus

Breakfast—pureed pears or pear chunks.

Lunch—steamed asparagus (or vegetable in season) pureed, or in small pieces.

Dinner—mashed banana.

Breastmilk on demand. Diluted, fresh orange or apple juice between meals, but not too close to vegetable meal.

The following are for use after several foods have been tested, and Baby shows no allergies in the first year, as well as enough teeth to chew small pieces of raw foods.

Breakfast—banana-apple puree, pear-apple puree, apple-apricot puree, or mixed fruit salad of similar fruits.

Lunch—piece of cucumber, steamed carrots mashed and then sliced, steamed yellow squash mashed and then sliced.

Dinner—avocado mashed with tomato, steamed mung bean sprouts.

Breastmilk on demand. Juice as snack. Hard carrot for teething.

The following are for use after grains are introduced and tested for allergies. By now many fruits and vegetables will have been tested for allergies. Mixed foods are permissible, but stick to simple combinations that promote digestion. If you are no longer breastfeeding, or if there is very little breastfeeding, you might want to try homemade, unsweetened yogurt or raw cow's or goat's milk, preferably in a pre-digested state such as yogurt, buttermilk, cottage cheese, or kefir.

Breakfast—plain yogurt with acidic fruit (berries, pineapple, oranges) or eggs with alfalfa sprouts.

Lunch—steamed green or yellow vegetables with brown rice, millet, buckwheat, or barley.

Dinner—either fruit meal (bananas with soaked dates) or grain meal (oatmeal). If grains are served at lunch, use fruit meal.

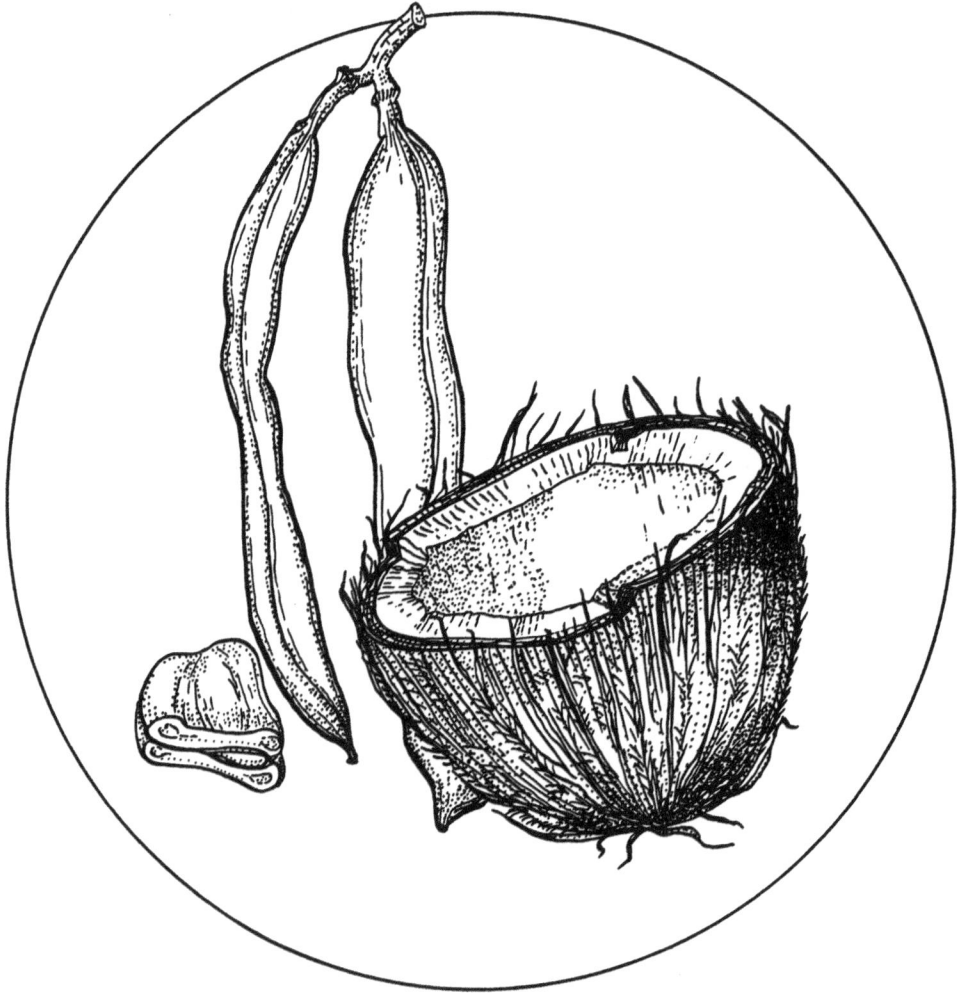

Chapter Eleven

Good Food for Special Problems

If you or your child suffer from food allergies, you're not alone. Foods like chocolate, cola, peanuts, eggs, corn, citrus fruits, and cereal grains are the most common allergies and, although they may be a regular part of some people's diet, to the allergic person, they're almost poison.

Allergies are often inherited traits, causing trouble from the time of infancy. They increase susceptibility to infection, and the victim will often suffer from Allergic Tension-Fatigue Syndrome. Besides fatigue, the main symptoms of this syndrome include: irritability, pale skin, circles under the eyes, stuffy nose, headache, and stomach and leg aches. Other symptoms are urinary problems, bowel disorders, and even behavior and learning problems.

Behavior changes caused by allergies range from hyperactivity to a withdrawn state, which may even approach autism. Both types of children, over-active and excessively withdrawn, respond poorly to stress: the withdrawn child retreats from environmental stimuli, while the hyperactive child overreacts physically. Parents with hyperactive children can consult local Feingold Associations, located throughout the United States. This parent association keeps a current list of recommended and off-limit foods and are supportive to all parents in their attempts to raise healthy, normally active youngsters.

In some instances, hyperactivity is not triggered by any specific food allergy. Processed foods containing synthetic (artificial) color or flavor, in combination with some fruits and vegetables containing natural salicylates, are the culprits. These salicylate fruits and vegetables, after being eliminated, can sometimes be gradually reintroduced into the diet without negative effects, so long as the artificials are avoided.

For the gluten-sensitive allergic child, bread and other grain products present seemingly insurmountable problems. Gluten products include wheat, rye, oats, and barley, although some people are allergic only to wheat or wheat and rye. Try to avoid processed or mixed foods which may not list trouble-making gluten ingredients in the manufacturer's formula. When you suspect an allergy as the cause of a behavior problem, I recommend altering your child's diet to exclude all the allergens, as well as any artificials, synthetics, and salicylates that can trigger hyperactive responses. Allergenic foods or food additives are occasionally hidden and have delayed reactions. In these cases, a special blood test performed by a clinical ecologist* may be necessary.

Your first question about an elimination diet may be: "What's left to eat?" Consider the wide variety of fresh foods in the vegetable kingdom, seeds and nuts, sprouts, and selected fruits. You may have to revert to the method you used when you first introduced your baby to solids—serve only one food at a time and watch for short and long-term reactions. It may not be easy, but this may be the only way to help your child develop a menu that will make him/her feel stronger, healthier, and happier. Keeping a food diary helps, or buy a notebook and start your own special diet recipe book.

If you or your child suffer from multiple food allergies, you may want to consider a food rotation diet. Each type of food is eaten only once every four to seven days, depending upon the plan you choose, and excepting fixed food allergies, which must be permanently eliminated. Rotation allows for greater flexibility than a straight elimination diet. The Special Problems Section in the Resource Chapter of this book lists several books written on rotation diets. Kits are also available, such as Sally Rockwell's The (Food) Rotation Game, or Jessica Denning's Rotating Meals on Wheels (see the Resource Listing under Special Problems). For more general information on clinical ecology write to HEAL—Human Ecology Action League, 505 Lake Shore Drive, Suite 6506, Chicago, IL 60611 or the Society for Clinical Ecology, 2005 Franklin, Suite 490, Denver, CO 80205. (Request the name of a clinical ecologist in your area.)

Treat food problems as a challenge rather than a chore and you'll find them less frustrating. A few culinary disasters are expected when you experiment. The peanut butter cookies will fall apart without the gluten, and your corn bread may look like corn bricks without the eggs. Keep trying and be positive. Preparing special foods for a special problem can bring out the creativity in a willing cook. Do share the resulting recipes with the whole family to make the suffering member feel less isolated. Consider allergy-free food preparation not as a kitchen handicap, but as a stepping stone to using whole, natural ingredients for a better family diet.

---

* Clinical Ecology, also known as Environmental Medicine, is a relatively new branch of medicine (25 years) which explores man's reaction to the environment. Because children and adults usually come to a specialist after symptoms appear, Clinical Ecology is not preventive, but once the problem has been diagnosed, appropriate methods can be used to prevent further health problems. If allergies run in the family, a clinical ecologist can provide a program to prevent their occurrence or lessen their severity.

The following recipes eliminate many common allergenic foods. Some may not be suitable for you or your child. You may have to make substitutions and manufacture your own allergy-free or anti-hyperactive recipes, or employ one of the ready-to-use diet rotation plans. All the dishes are made without additives or preservatives and can be given to a hyperactive child, unless they contain natural salicylate foods. (Many of the recipes from other sections of the book are suitable with regard to this chapter.)

Milk Substitutes

Soy milk is usually one of the common choices for children on milk-free diets. Several companies have recently introduced good-tasting soy milk sweetened lightly with honey, barley malt, or maple syrup. Soy milk is perfect as a substitute to cow's milk for children or adults who enjoy foods with milk but who are allergic to it. However, I prefer to use nut milks because they are tastier and easier to prepare. In fact, cashew milk looks much like regular milk. Banana and zucchini also work well as milks in recipes (see below).

Nut Milk

You can use sunflower seeds, blanched almonds, raw sesame seeds, or almost any raw nut of your choice. Use nut milks first in recipes and gradually include them in other parts of your diet, e.g. with cereal.

Soak 2/3 cup nuts in 1 quart water. Refrigerate overnight or for several hours. Next day, blend well and strain for smooth consistency. Use grindings in baking.

A quicker method: grind 2/3 cup broken cashews in a nut mill. Add 2 or 3 cups of water. The proportions depend on how thin a consistency you prefer, so experiment a little. Place ground nuts and water in the blender and buzz until smooth. Strain. Use as soon as possible. Keep refrigerated.

You can add a little extract and/or a dash of maple syrup for flavor. For chocolate-like flavor, add one or two Tablespoons of unsweetened carob flour to blender.

Banana Milk

Peel and puree a ripe banana with juice or water to a milky consistency. Use in recipes where sweet flavor is desired. (Example: smoothies, cookies.)

*Z*ucchini Milk
Peel and puree ripe zucchini with a small amount of water to a milk consistency. Use in preparing soups, breads, or vegetable sauces.

*E*gg Substitutes

These first two substitutions are reprinted with permission from Hanna Kroeger's Allergy Baking Recipes.

a. Soak 1/2 pound apricots in 2 cups water overnight. Next morning, beat or blend (add water if needed), strain, and store in refrigerator. Every time your recipe calls for beaten eggs, take a generous Tablespoon of this and blend into your dough.

b. To 3 cups of cold water add 1 cup ground flaxseed. Bring to a boil, stirring constantly. Boil for 3 minutes. Cool. Place in the refrigerator in a closed jar.

Whenever your recipe calls for 1 beaten egg, substitute 1 Tablespoon of mixture; for 2 eggs, take 2 Tablespoons, etc. You can make all types of pancakes, muffins, and cookies by substituting flaxseed recipe for given eggs.

The following recipes are reprinted with permission from free-lance writer Fran Goulart, author of Eating to Win, Bon Appetit, Cooking with Carob, the Vegetarian Weight Loss Cookbook, etc.

a. Any sort of cooked pureed bean paste will replace an egg in any bread recipe.

b. Soy Lecithin: a flake or granule, nutty and nice tasting, extracted from soybeans. Smoothes and emulsifies sauces, gravies, and creams. When making batters for baked goods, leave out the egg, and add one teaspoon lecithin for each pound of batter, roughly.

c. Potato and Arrowroot Starch (flour): Make a smooth paste out of 1 teaspoon of whichever you prefer, combined with 1/2 cup warm water (twice as much for potato starch). Even better and more binding with 1 teaspoon of soyflour and a pinch of lecithin, too. Use to replace the beaten egg in main dishes (casseroles, one-dish dishes, etc.). Sauces too.

d. Nuts and Seeds: Linseed and flaxseed are the most gelatinous and binding (they can be laxatives too, so look out), but any nut or seed properly pulverized (via rolling pin, seed mill, or blender) will produce an oily cream and, together with some liquid, will make a paste with the thickening power of one or more eggs. Experiment with different nuts, seeds, and fluids. Finely crushed peanuts, broth, cayenne, and coriander; soy sauce and vegetable stock, apple cider and pine nuts, etc. (For dinner and dessert gravies and sauces.)

e. A Tablespoon of quick-cooking tapioca in place of an egg in a thick sauce, gravy, or cooked dessert, will "get it together," too.

f. Eggless mayonnaise: liquefy or beat ripe banana, add oil until thickened. Add lemon juice to taste.

Uncooked Carob Icing

Ingredients

1/4 cup tahini (sesame paste)
1/4 cup maple syrup or honey
1/2 cup carob
1/4 cup water (approximately)
Juice of 1/2 lemon

Preparation

Cream tahini and maple syrup in bowl. Mix carob, water, and lemon juice in another bowl. Mix the two together thoroughly until creamy and smooth. Excess can be refrigerated, but bring to room temperature before using again and add a drop or two of water if necessary.

Nut 'n' Seed Cereal

Ingredients

Almonds
Cashews
Sunflower seeds
Pumpkin seeds

Preparation

Use unsalted seeds and nuts. Grind and place in bowl. Eat with fruit juice or nut milk.

Pseudo-Succotash

Ingredients

1 lb. yellow split peas (2 cups)
4 cups water
2 cups frozen lima beans (fresh when in season)
2-3 chopped scallions (optional)
1/2 chopped bell pepper (optional)
Herbs to taste

Preparation

Cook peas in water over medium heat for about 25-30 minutes. (Tender, but not mushy.) Reserve 1 cup peas and set aside to cool. Add lima beans to pot and cook about 10 minutes more or until peas and beans are soft. Puree the reserved cup of cooled yellow peas in blender, adding a little water if necessary. If you use them, saute scallions and pepper in small amount of water or oil while peas and beans cook. Add pureed peas back to pot along with sauteed scallions and pepper, if used. Gently stir in spices to taste. Serve in an attractive dish, hot or cold.

Hawaiian Snowballs

Ingredients

1/2 pound dried pineapple pieces (no sugar added)
2 ounces, or about 1/2 cup, raw almonds
Dash of almond extract
Coconut for rolling and covering balls (dried and unsweetened)

Preparation

Grind pineapple alternately with almonds in a hand grinder. When all the nuts and pineapple are ground, add a dash of almond extract. Then mix as thoroughly as possible. (The mixture will be stiff.) Roll into balls, using your hands. Then roll in coconut. Place on a cookie sheet in the refrigerator for a few minutes, or serve as is.

Note

Depending on the size of the balls, you can get one, two, or three dozen. These are very sweet, so use them sparingly.

Mary's Tofu Eggless Salad

Ingredients

1 block Tofu, drained well and cubed
2-3 stalks chopped celery
1/2 cup onion, chopped
Hain's eggless mayonnaise (available at natural food stores) or Tofunnaise (see recipe below)
Bread

Preparation

Toss all ingredients and mash with a fork to spread on bread. For an eggier color, add some turmeric.

Tofunnaise Dressing

Ingredients

1/4 cup water
1 T. oil
Juice of 1/2 lemon
1/2 t. natural soy sauce (optional)
4 ounces firm, drained tofu, cut into pieces
1/2 t. turmeric (optional for color)

Preparation

Place ingredients in blender in order listed. Puree until smooth. Yields about 3/4 cup dressing.

Note

Dressing tends to thicken upon refrigeration. You may need to mix in additional water if used the following day.

Guacamole

Ingredients

2 very ripe avocados 1 medium-sized fresh tomato
1 small onion, chopped (about 1/2 cup)
2 teaspoons lemon juice
1 or 2 teaspoons chili powder (optional or omit, especially for children)

Preparation

Peel avocados and mash pulp, leaving a few lumps throughout. Peel and chop tomato and add to avocado. Add onion, lemon juice, and seasonings to taste. If not used immediately, refrigerate in a covered bowl, with pit immersed in dip. (helps prevent discoloration). Serve as a salad on lettuce, as a dip with raw veggies, or as a condiment to top taco fillings. For a smoother guacamole, use blender or food processor.

Gazpacho

No gluten, eggs, or dairy.

Ingredients (List 1)

1/2 cucumber, peeled if waxed, then cut into chunks
2-3 chopped tomatoes 2 lemons, juiced
1/2 cup tomato juice or vegetable juice
1 Tablespoon olive oil (optional)
1/4 teaspoon oregano
1/2 teaspoon kelp
2 garlic cloves, peeled

Preparation

Puree in blender.

Ingredients (List 2) — Any or All

Sliced scallions
Chopped or diced cucumber
Diced celery
Chopped parsley
Chopped string beans or yellow squash

Preparation

Add to pureed vegetables. Thin with tomato or vegetable juice to desired consistency and serve chilled.

Coconut-Banana Bread

No gluten, eggs, or dairy.

Dry Ingredients

2 cups millet flour
2 cups soy flour or corn meal
1 Tablespoon aluminum-free baking powder
1/2 cup dried, unsweetened coconut
1 Tablespoon allspice

Wet Ingredients

1 cup safflower oil
1/2 cup honey, sorghum, or barley-malt syrup
1/2 cup water or unsweetened juice
3 ripe bananas

Preparation

Mix dry ingredients in a large bowl. Blend wet ingredients in blender or by hand. Combine wet ingredients with dry ingredients and mix well.

Pour into a well-oiled 8"x 8" bake pan or small loaf pan, and bake in a 350° pre-heated oven for about 45 minutes. (The shallow bake pan should take less time than the loaf pan, so check with a toothpick at about 30 minutes to determine if bake pan cake is done.)

Vegetable Lentil Soup

Ingredients (no dairy, wheat, or eggs)

1 or 2 scrubbed and sliced carrots
2 or 3 potatoes, scrubbed and cubed
3/4 pound of dry brown lentils, soaked overnight or for several hours in more than enough water to cover. (Lentils absorb a lot of water.)
6 cups water or stock
1 onion
1 garlic clove
1 bay leaf Sprig of parsley
2 or 3 scrubbed celery stalks, with tops
Spices to taste—basil, oregano, thyme, kelp

Marusan's wheat-free soy sauce (optional)
1 or 2 cups cooked beans, noodles, or grain, such as rice (optional)

Preparation

Steam or cook carrots and potatoes until almost tender. In the meantime, drain soaked lentils (discard soaking water), and mix with 6 cups water or stock in a large pot. Add onion, garlic clove, bay leaf, parsley, and celery stalks and bring to a slow boil over medium heat. Reduce heat and simmer about 15 minutes, or until lentils are soft. Add tender carrots and potatoes to simmering lentils. Spice to taste and cook slowly for another fifteen minutes to allow flavors to mingle and potatoes and carrots to become tender.

Remove onion, garlic, bay leaf, parsley, and celery, and soup is ready to serve. Serve with croutons or sprouts. If you wish, add one or two cups of cooked rice, noodles, or beans. This will make the soup thick, and you may wish to add some additional water or stock.

Simpler method: Add all ingredients to water and simmer until lentils and vegetables are tender, adding cooked beans or rice at end, after removing onions, garlic, parsley, etc.

Note

Soaking water makes great food for your plants.

Creamy, Yellow Pea Soup

Ingredients (no wheat, eggs, or dairy)

6 cups water*
2 cups yellow split peas
1 or 2 potatoes
1 onion
1 garlic clove
Celery leaves
Fresh parsley
1 grated carrot
Spices or herbs of your choice (ex. curry powder)
Marusan's wheat-free natural soy sauce (optional)

Preparation

Place water, split peas, onion, garlic, celery leaves, potatoes, fresh parsley, and herbs in large pot and bring to a boil. Then turn to simmer for about 1/2 hour. In the meantime, grate the carrots and set them aside.

When peas and potatoes are soft enough to eat, remove pot from stove and let cool a few minutes. Then puree almost all the peas and potatoes with the remaining water, removing parsley, garlic, and onion if you wish. For creamier soup, puree all potatoes and peas. Put soup back on stove, and add carrots. Simmer a few minutes more, adding additional spices and herbs if necessary for flavor. Serve with popcorn croutons.

* Very thick with 6 cups water. Add more water for thinner consistency.

Variations

Add corn kernels, whole peas, chickpeas (cooked) or other vegetable of your choice. Right before serving, sprinkle in some freshly sprouted lentils.

Corn Taco Stuffing

Ingredients (no wheat, dairy, or eggs)

4 cups cooked beans (pinto or kidney)
2 tomatoes, chopped
1/2 cup chopped walnuts (optional)
Dash of chili powder or garlic powder

Preparation

Puree in blender or mash to a thick consistency, using water from cooked beans. Add only enough liquid to puree. Lumps O.K. Add a dash of chili powder, garlic powder, and cayenne to taste. For true red color, use kidney beans; pinto comes out pink. Stuffing should be a thick consistency. Use as filling in corn tacos.

Note

May be used as a dip when chilled.

Banana/Avocado Pudding

Ingredients

1/2 pound ripe avocado (1 medium)
1/2 pound ripe banana (2-3)
1/2 cup apple juice
1/2 cup carob (unsweetened)

Preparation

Blend apple juice and carob on low speed. Add peeled and chopped avocado and banana, a little at a time. For thinner consistency, add more juice. Refrigerate. Right before serving, sprinkle with your favorite natural topping—bee pollen, date powder, coconut, carob chips.

This recipe works best as a breakfast pudding.

Molly's Pancake Patties

Ingredients (no gluten, dairy, or eggs)

1 - 1 1/4 cups water or Juice*
1/4 cup tahini or peanut butter
2 T. safflower oil
1 cup allowable flour (rice, millet, buckwheat, arrowroot)
1 T. cereal-free baking powder **
1 t. allspice

Preparation

Preheat fry pan while mixing the ingredients. Blend first three ingredients in blender on medium speed. Mix flour, baking powder, and allspice, adding to blender a little bit at a time.

Pour a small amount of oil or butter in fry pan and pour batter from blender into pan, making small pancakes about 3-4 inches in diameter. When bubbles form on the edges, flip over and cook until brown. Remove and drain on paper towels. Serve hot with your favorite topping. Serve cold as "pancake buns" in place of bread. Refrigerate or freeze with wax paper between each pancake. Yields 12-15 pancakes.

Note
If you're using a cast-iron fry pan, oil or butter is not really necessary.

* For thinner pancakes, not "buns," use more water. For thicker, more doughy pancakes, use less water. Thicker pancakes are better for bread "cakes."
** Available from Walnut Acres. (See Mail Order List.)

Mock Mocha/Malt Syrup

Ingredients

1 cup water
1/4 cup carob powder, lightly toasted
1/4 cup Cafix, Postum, or other grain beverage
1 cup malt powder
1/4 cup date powder, ground finely

Preparation

Dissolve carob and Cafix in almost boiling water. Reduce heat gradually. Whisk in malt and date powder, stirring to a smooth consistency. Pour hot over desserts or use cold as a chocolate milk substitute.

Naturally Sweet Caroballs

Dry Ingredients

1/4 cup carob powder (unsweetened)
1/2 cup soy milk powder or protein powder (unsweetened and non-dairy)

Wet Ingredients

1/2 Tablespoon safflower oil
1 cup peanut butter (natural)
2 ripe bananas
1/8 - /14 cup apple juice

Optional

Vanilla extract or almond extract
Raisins
Nuts

Coconuts
Sesame seeds
Preparation

Mix wet ingredients in one bowl. Mix dry ingredients in another bowl. Add wet to dry, using enough apple juice to make a fudge-like consistency.

Oil hands and form mixture into ping-pong sized balls, then roll the balls in coconut (unsweetened) or sesame seeds. Feel free to add any of the optional ingredients, keeping in mind that dried fruit and nuts are nutritious, but also high in calories. Makes about 2 dozen...Eat with discretion.

Note

May be suitable for diabetes-prone children. Check with your doctor.

Carobana Malt

Ingredients

1 T. carob powder
1 T. malt
1 T. banana flakes (or 1/2 banana)
1 cup milk (soy, coconut, or nut milk)

Preparation

Buzz all ingredients in the blender. (Note: This drink can be served cold or heated over a low flame.)

Variation

For those allergic to milk, use 1 cup nut milk with 1 T. Protein Powder. (Nut milk: soak 2/3 c. nuts in 1 qt. water overnight. Blend, strain, and drink.)

Tropical Popsicle

Ingredients

1/2 cup unsweetened pineapple juice
3 ripe bananas (sliced)
1 cup drained, crushed pineapple (packed in own juice)
1/4 cup date sugar dissolved in 1/2 cup hot water
Dash orange extract (optional)
1/2 cup dried, unsweetened coconut

Preparation

Place juice, bananas, pineapple, and dissolved date sugar in blender or food processor and blend until smooth. Add extract and coconut and stir by hand. Pour into popsicle molds, or paper cups, with pop sticks. (Partially freeze before adding your own sticks.) Freeze. Yield almost 3 cups.

Note

Any leftovers can be used as a sauce over fruit salad if more juice is added.

Bananas on a Stick 2

Ingredients (no dairy or sugar)

1/3 cup tahini (sesame paste)
1/3 cup thick juice, like pina colada
3 bananas, cut into thirds crosswise
Coating: coconut, date powder, granola, sesame seeds

Preparation

Hand blend tahini and juice in bowl to a thick, sauce-like consistency. With fingers or tongs, dip cut bananas into sauce, covering completely. Roll any of the coatings, pierce broadside of coated banana with toothpick, place in cupcake papers, or on cookie sheet, and freeze. Thaw slightly before serving. (This can be a good project for children—messy, but fun, and teaches that treats need not be highly sweetened.)

Chapter Twelve

Odds and Ends

The recipes in this section do not fit smoothly into any of the other chapters. They can be used at breakfast, for snacks, as lunch bag tuck-ins, or whatever strikes your fancy. Enjoy!

Sharon's Sun Tea

Ingredients

1/4 to 1/2 cup dried herb leaves (double for fresh leaves)
2 quarts fresh spring water
Mint leaves (optional)

Preparation

Place herbal tea leaves in the bottom of a 2 quart jar, more or less according to taste. (Try mint and orange peel, teaberry, or your own favorite.) Pour in fresh water almost to the top. Add some fresh mint leaves if available. Cover jar with cheesecloth and place in direct sunlight for at least 2 hours. Strain, refrigerate, and serve. Easy, refreshing, and delicious. (Add more water to tea if too strong.)

Sparkling "Soda" Water

Ingredients

1 large bottle naturally sparkling mineral water (23 oz.)
2 Tablespoons cherry juice concentrate (no sugar)
Dash lemon juice

Preparation

Add cherry concentrate and lemon to chilled sparkling water and serve like soda.

Grape Soda

Ingredients

8 oz. sparkling water or Seltzer without preservatives
4 oz. unsweetened Grape Juice, chilled

Preparation

Combine and serve.

Fruit Punch

Ingredients

1 qt. apple juice
1 qt. grape juice
1 qt. pear juice
1 qt. pineapple or cranberry juice
Fresh fruit and berry slices

Preparation

Mix together in large bowl and add slices of fresh fruit or berries on top. (Use fruit in season or unsweetened frozen fruit.)

Sunburst Dip with Fruit

Ingredients

1 ripe pineapple
1 papaya or cantaloupe
1 or 2 oranges or grapefruit
1 pint ripe strawberries
1 or 2 red Delicious apples
1 or 2 yellow Delicious apples
Lemon yogurt (without sugar or preservatives)
Maple syrup (optional)

Preparation

Peel and slice pineapple into thick chunks. Cut papaya lengthwise, scoop out seeds, peel, and cut into chunks. Or use a melon bailer and make papaya balls. Peel oranges and divide into whole slices with the membranes intact. Wash strawberries and leave whole. Wash and cut apples into bite sized wedges. Sprinkle with lemon to prevent discoloration. (You may want to prepare these last if no lemon is available.)

Place lemon yogurt (with a dash of maple syrup, if you wish) in a small deep bowl in the center of a large platter. Arrange cut fruit in rays around the center, radiating from the bowl of yogurt dip. Alternate red and yellow fruits so that the finished dish is attractive. Place pineapple chunks in a wedge covering 11 to 1 o'clock, strawberries from 1 to 3 o'clock, yellow apples from 3 to 5 o'clock, pineapple again from 5 to 7 o'clock, dried apples from 7 to 9 o'clock, and papaya from 9 to 11 o'clock.

Serve immediately with bamboo skewers or toothpicks for dipping fruits into dip. A delicious dish anytime.

Sweet Potato-Avocado Dip

Ingredients

1-2 cooked sweet potatoes, skins removed
1 ripe avocado
Spices and seed to taste

Preparation

Mash potatoes and avocado together with a fork, pastry blender, or potato masher until smooth. Add spices to taste: for Indian flavor, use curry powder; for Italian flavor, use oregano and garlic; for Oriental flavor, add soy sauce and black sesame seeds; for crunchy flavor, add caraway and sesame seeds or ground walnuts. Use as a spread or dip with pita bread, crackers, or celery.

Variation

Substitute yogurt for avocado for a creamier, lighter taste.

Sunburst Dip with Vegetables

Ingredients (List 1)

1 or 2 carrots
1 bunch red radishes
1 small yellow squash or yellow turnip
1 pint cherry tomatoes
1 small cauliflower
14 pound mushrooms

Preparation

Scrub carrots and cut into thick "pennies" (crosswise cut) Scrub radishes and trim. Scrub squash or turnip and cut into bite-sized chunks. Rinse cherry tomatoes and remove stems. Wash cauliflower and break into flowerettes. Wash mushrooms with a wet paper towel (don't soak) and cut lengthwise into thick pieces.

Ingredients (List 2)

1/2 pound Ricotta cheese or drained, firm tofu (soy bean cheese)
Juice of 1/2 lemon
1/2 to 1 cup tahini sesame paste
Natural soy sauce (optional)
Garlic powder
Turmeric or curry powder

Preparation

Place the cheese or tofu and lemon juice in the blender. Blend thoroughly, adding a little water if necessary. Remove cheese from blender and place in a bowl. Mix in tahini by hand (more or less according to taste). Add a dash of natural soy sauce and garlic powder. Sprinkle on some turmeric or curry powder. This will give the dip a yellow color and added flavor.

Place sundip in a small, deep bowl in the center of a large platter. Arrange vegetables in rays around the dip. Alternate red, yellow, and white vegetables around the center like rays of the sun. Imagine the dish as a clock. Place cherry tomatoes from 11 to 1 o'clock, mushrooms from 1 to 3 o'clock, carrots from 3 to 5 o'clock, yellow squash or turnips from 5 to 7 o'clock, radishes from 7 to 9 o'clock, and cauliflower from 9 to 11 o'clock.

Variations

Feel free to use any other vegetables that are in season or that are your favorites. Be creative.

Vegipasto

Ingredients

Carrots
Celery
Bell Peppers (red and green)
Avocado (ripe)
Tomatoes
Cucumber or zucchini
Yellow squash
Olives (optional)
Cheese chunks (optional)

Preparation

Scrub carrots and cut into lengthwise strips. Scrub celery and cut crosswise into 3-4" pieces. Wash and scrub bell peppers and cut into rings or strips. Peel avocado and cut into slivers or chunks. Slice the tomatoes or cut them into wedges. Clean and slice the cucumbers or zucchini and the squash. Rinse and drain olives and place in a bowl temporarily. Cut cheese into chunks.

On a large platter, arrange the vegetables. Put toothpicks through olives and then through cheese chunks. Put carrot and celery sticks in center and arrange the sliced and wedged veggies around them, or place celery and carrots like spokes on a wheel and arrange other veggies in between. Alternate the different colors so that red tomato is not next to another red food. Serve plain or spritzed with a little lemon juice, especially on the avocado. Feel free to add whole wheat bread sticks or bread slices, deli-size bread slices, or whole wheat pita wedges.

Fruit Soup

Ingredients

Bite-sized dried fruits of your choice (unsulfured)
Apple juice
Fresh apple
Ripe banana
Optional: Raisins, applesauce, cinnamon stick

Preparation

Soak unsulfured dried fruit pieces (peaches, pears, apricots, pitted dates) in apple juice, with more than enough juice to allow fruit to be reconstituted. Refrigerate soaking fruit, adding more apple juice if necessary to reach a "soupy" consistency. You may also add a stick of cinnamon for extra flavor. Right before serving, dice in a fresh apple and add some ripe banana slices. Sprinkle on some raisins or a dollop of applesauce.

Note

Dried fruit (although natural) is high in concentrated sweetness, so brush your teeth soon after eating.

Parsley-Garlic-Walnut Dressing

Ingredients

1/2 cup olive or safflower oil
Juice of one lemon
1 Tablespoon fresh parsley or 1/2 Tablespoon dried parsley
    flakes
2 minced garlic cloves
1/4 cup chopped walnuts
Dash of oregano and basil
1/2 cup water
1 teaspoon honey (optional)

Preparation

Place all ingredients in the blender and blend until nuts are small. To thicken, add 2 to 3 Tablespoons of tahini (sesame paste) by hand after removing mixture from blender.

Alfa - Dressing

Ingredients

1 cup natural mayonnaise
1 minced garlic clove
1 or 2 minced parsley leaves or dried parsley flakes
1 teaspoon natural soy sauce (optional)
1 or 2 minced green onions
1/2 cup alfalfa sprouts

Preparation

Place all in the blender and whir for a few seconds. For thicker dressing, mix in 1 Tablespoon mayonnaise by hand after removing mixture from blender. Shake well before serving over salad.

Variation

Substitute one cup plain yogurt or tofu plus one or two teaspoons honey. For greener dressing, add more parsley flakes.

Ambrosia Fruit Salad

Ingredients

1 fresh pineapple
3 tangerines or oranges
1 grapefruit
Orange or pineapple juice
Unsweetened grated coconut (dried or fresh) or almond slivers

Preparation

Cut pineapple into chunks, peel oranges and grapefruit, and separate into sections. Place in a bowl with juice. Sprinkle with coconut or almonds and serve. Simple, but attractive and tasty.

Travel Munchies

Ingredients

1/2 pound unsalted sesame sticks or unsalted pretzel sticks (whole wheat)*
1/2 pound unsulfured raisins
3/4 pound unsalted peanuts
3/4 pound unsalted, hulled sunflower seeds

Preparation

Mix all ingredients in a bowl. Place in individual cellophane, paper bag or in paper cups for each child. Great for munching on the road.

* Use puffed corn or puffed rice for wheat-sensitive munchers.

Chapter Thirteen

Resource List: Where to Go From Here

These books helped me formulate a good food program for my family. Each book listed contains some worthwhile information, even though each author has his or her own individual food philosophy. Eventually you will develop the plan that works bests for you and your family. These books should help you find your plan. Read with enthusiasm and an open mind, and you will benefit from all of them. Out-of-print books may still be available at your library.

The starred books comprise the bibliography of this book.

New Edition Notes: In the 25 years since this book was published, many more books have been written and circulated. I have eliminated books from the original list that I feel are no longer applicable or are out of print. With the Internet, books are being replaced by websites, so there will be fewer books in this list. The best way to find a book is to Google the title or the topic, or go to one of the book websites, such as Amazon.com or Border.com and type in the topic. The somewhat shortened list below represents books that have helped me maintain a whole feeds food plan. This is therefore a personal list, not a comprehensive list. I checked the older ones I kept to see if they were still available and noted this with a +. They can be found new and/or used at www.Amazon.com , www.alibris.com, www. barnesandnoble.com, or www.borders.com.

In some cases, the publisher has changed and in other I could not find the new publisher, so please use the author and title as your guide.

*Again, the starred books comprise the bibliography/resources I used to write it, so these books have been left on the list, even if they are out of print. (Some may still be available as used books. I added a + to the *.*

+Airola, Paavo, Ph.D., M.D. *Are You Confused?* Arizona: Health Plus Publishers, 1971.

For those who need help with the contradictions in natural foods, food cures, herbs, vitamins, etc. Includes simple, wholesome recipes and information on fasting. Good reference/resource book.

Rating: Very good

*+Airola, Paavo. *Everywoman's Book,* Phoenix, Arizona: Health Plus Pub.

A comprehensive, holistic health guide covering three main areas:

Mothering, Children's Health, and Specific Female Problems. Easy to read, complete, and informative. Good reference book as well as general guide for women.

Rating: Very good to Excellent

+Blue Goose, Inc. *The Buying Guide for Fresh Fruits, Vegetables, Herbs, and Nuts, California*: Blue Goose, Inc., 1974.

I found this book at the supermarket being used by the produce manager. All the different fruits and vegetables are described and important information about each of them is given. A great guide for the shopper.

Rating; Very good

Bowden, Jonny. *The 150 Healthiest Foods on Earth*. Massachusetts: Fair Winds Press, 2007.

A beautifully illustrated, large (81/2" X 11") book that covers super foods from every category: Beans & Beverages to Specialty Foods & Oils. Easy to read with stars on the foods that are extra-super healthy.

Rating: Excellent!

*+Burkett, Denis. *Eat Right to Stay Healthy and Enjoy Life More,* New York: Ar-co Publishing Co., 1979.

An easy-to-ready, informative book explaining the relationship between low fiber diets and so called degenerative diseases prevalent in "civilized" countries.`Clear, factual, and revealing.

Rating: Excellent

+Carroll, Anstice and DePersiis Vona, Embree. *The Health Food Dictionary with Recipes,* New Jersey: Prentice Hall, 1973.

A beautifully illustrated, alphabetical, natural foods book that I use constantly. There are many recipes included within the definitions. A book I wouldn't do without.

Rating: Excellent

Charney, Steve & Goldbeck, David. *The ABC's of Fruits and Vegetables and Beyond*. Woodstock, NY: Ceres Press, 2007.

A delightful book that is educational, enjoyable, and easy-to-read for kids. The first half is food alphabet using Rhymes. The second half takes these same foods and provides facts, recipes, jokes, and children's books related to that food or food concept. Graphics are wonderful! Perfect way to get kids to learn about good foods.

Rating: Excellent

Editors of Prevention Magazine. *The Complete Book of Alternative Nutrition*. PA: Rodale Press, 1997.

Subtitled "Powerful New Ways to Use Foods, Supplements, Herbs and Special Diets to Prevent and Cure Disease." If you are interested in alternative ways to stay healthy with special diets, such as ayurveda, macrobiotics, raw foods, etc., this is a good overview. (No recipes)

Rating: Good to Very Good

*+Goldbeck, Nikki and Goldbeck, David. *The Supermarket Handbook*, New York: Signet Books, 1973.

A worthwhile resource book for every serious shopper. The Goldbecks have scoured the supermarket to find the best nutritional buys in the store. A real help to parents seeking whole foods among the maze of "non-foods" in the supermarket. Natural food recipes included.

Rating: Excellent

Heinerman, John. *Heinerman's New Encyclopedia of Fruits & Vegetables*. West Nyack, NY: Parker Publishing Co., 1995. (Available used from Amazon. com)

A comprehensive, 504-page guide to health symptoms and their food remedies, from arthritis to zucchini, including recipes to eat as well as recipes for use on the skin. No pictures, but filled with information.

Rating: Very Good

*+Hunter, Beatrice Trum. Fact Book on Food Additives and Your Health, New Canaan, CT: Keats Pub. Co., 1972.

A handy guide starting with facts and types of food additives followed by some individual common additives and how they affect the body.

Rating: Very good

Kirschmann, John D. *Nutrition Almanac*, New York: McGraw Hill Book Company, 1973.

A handy reference book that includes all the nutrients our bodies need, common ailments and treatment suggestions, table of food composition (calories, water, vitamins, and minerals), and basic information on nutrition and health.

Rating: Excellent

*Kloss, Jethro. *Back to Eden*, California: Back to Eden Books, 1982.

Considered the Herbal Bible by many. Contains valuable information on good nutrition, fasting, proper cooking methods, utensils, special treatments for different ailments, and recipes. Includes an extensive alphabetical listing of herbs.

Rating: Excellent

Nestle, Marion. *What to Eat: An Aisle-by-Aisle Guide to Savvy Food Choices and Good Eating*. New York: Farrar, Strauss, & Giroux. 2006.

A comprehensive book that explores important areas of our food, including frozen and fresh, organic vs. conventional food, food safety, and more.

Rating: Very good.

+Peterson, Vicki. *The Natural Food Catalog*, New York: Arco Publishing Company, Inc.1978.

A complete alphabetical listing of whole foods. Chapters on herbs and spices, beverages, kitchen utensils, gardening, and additives. A good all-around natural foods catalog with sketches, photographs, and recipes.

Rating: Very good

Planck, Nina. *Real Food: What to Eat and Why*. New York: Bloomsbury Books, 2006.

An interesting "menu memoir" in which the author, who grew up on a farm explains the difference between real food and manufactured food, how she lost her way and came back to real food. There are no recipes or pictures, but her story is a good place to begin learning about a wholesome diet. Helpful

resources & Glossary at the end of the book.
Rating: Good to Very good

Pollan Michael. *In Defense of Food*. A slim volume with a simple message: "Eat (Real) Food. Not too Much." Mostly Plants. But while the message is simple, learning to eat this way has become a problem because of so much processed food.
Rating: Very good

Rinzler, Carol Ann. *The Complete Book of Food: A Nutritional, Medical, & Culinary Guide.* Facts on File, Inc., 2009 (2nd edition).
Nutritionist Jane Brody notes in the Introduction that this book is a must for those who want to get the most from the food they eat, as well as avoid dietary pitfalls. This comprehensive guide does just that.
Rating: Very good

Schlosser, Eric. *Fast Food Nation*. New York, Houghton Mifflin Co., 2001.
A searing critique of the rise of fast foods in postwar (WWII) America. Eye-opening, upsetting, and thought provoking. Anyone concerned about the state of food landscape must read this.
Rating: Excellent

+Seidman, Susan and Kennedy, Sheila. *Working Family's Kitchen Guide*, California: 101 Productions, 1980.
Comprehensive guidebook for busy families. Natural foods recipes comprise the book's second half. Includes helpful cooking and shopping hints, menu planning, shopping and cooking with children, and eating out. Some questionable ingredients. Substitutions can easily be made.
Rating: Very good

*+Shelton, Herbert M. *Food Combining Made Easy*, Texas: Dr. Shelton's Health School, 1977.
Basic book for those concerned with natural hygiene. Sample menus included.
Rating: Very good

*+Tomlinson, H., Aluminum *Utensils and Disease*, London: LN Fowler and Co., 1972. *Tomlinson, H., Aluminum Utensils and Disease, London: LN Fowler and Co., 1972.

A brief, but powerful, book linking aluminum sensitivity to several health problems. Based on personal experiences, the argument the author makes is convincing.

Rating: Very good

Zinczenco, David. *Eat This, Not That*. PA: Rodale Press. 2000+ A series of five (so far) reference books covering a wide range of topics from kids' diets to surviving in the supermarket to weight loss. Common sense information. A good place to begin if you are confused about foods to buy for you and your family. Actual images of products fill the small pages with excellent nutritional information. Check out the website: www.eatthis.com

Rating: Very good to Excellent

Food Books For Moms, Babies, & Youngsters

+deBairacli-Levy, Juliette. *Nature's Children*, New York: Schocken Books, 1971.

An herbal approach to child rearing. Includes information on health of parents, birth, breastfeeding, and nature's medicines. Natural remedies listed alphabetically. Also includes recipes. This is worthwhile reading, although some of the recipes contain sugar and salt.

Rating: Very good

+Baxter, Kathleen. *Come and Get It*, Ann Arbor, MI: Children First Press, 1981.

This spiral bound, natural foods cookbook for children has colored pages and hand-printed recipes. Recipe book is interesting and includes beverages, desserts, salads, breads, and dishes for each meal. Recipes do use small amounts of salt, pepper, and condiments like mustard, but these can be omitted or substituted.

Rating: Good

*+Bircher-Benner, M., M.D. *Children's Diet Book*, Connecticut: Keats Publishing, Inc., 1977.

A nutritious children's book that pulls no punches about what's good for your kids. Should also be read by parents-to-be, teachers, and nutritionists. Includes sample menus and recipes from basic whole foods.

Rating: Very good

+*The Boston Women's Health Book Collective. Our Bodies, Ourselves*, New York: Simon &.Schuster, 1979.

The childbearing unit of this large book is important reading for both mothers and fathers-to-be. Valuable physical (including nutritional) and emotional information on pre-conception, pregnancy, and post-partum periods. Sensitive and sensible treatment of the entire subject of parenthood.

Rating: Very good

The Children's Foundation. *Eating Better at School*, New York: Center for Science in the Public Interest, Washington D.C., and The Children's Foundation, 1980.

Guide for parents, educators, and other adults concerned with better cafeteria food for children. Perfect for groups wanting to improve school lunch programs.

Rating: Very good

Note: This book has been replaced by CSPI's website with updated school nutrition programs. Go to: http://www.cspinet.org/nutritionpolicy/nana.html

+Cooper, Jane. *Love at First Bite*, New York: Alfred Knopf, 1977.

A cleverly illustrated children's cookbook. Chapters on breakfast^ lunch, snacks, desserts, and drinks, as well as sections on necessary kitchen equipment and preparation hints for the natural food recipes.

Rating: Very good

+Elliot, Sharon. *Dinner Can Be A Picnic All Year Round*, California: Fresh Press, 1981.

Based on the idea that picnics are special, recipes make mealtimes more like picnics. Easy to read and easy to follow recipes. Some use salt. Variety and imaginative variations give this book a special flavor suitable for teenagers as well as adults.

Rating: Very good

+Farmilant, Eunice. *The 'Natural Sweet-Tooth Cookbook*, New York: Jove Publications, 1978.

My favorite dessert cookbook. No sugar of any kind is used, and this includes honey, sorghum, etc. Author relies on dried fruit, juices, teas, and toasted grains for sweeteners. Some recipes take a little more time, but the sugarless rewards are worth it. Recipes may be suitable for diabetics, but check with your doctor first.

Rating: Excellent

+Elam, Daniel. *Building Better Babies*, California: Celestial Alts, 1980.
An excellent and easily understood physiological overview of the human reproduction system. Healthy mothers and fathers are emphasized as prerequisites to healthy offspring. A must reading for parents-to-be.
Rating: Excellent

Franklin, Emily. *Too Many Cooks*. New York: Hyperion, 2009.
Subtitled "Mom, 4 Kids, and 102 Recipes," this is not so much a cookbook as a memoir with seasonal recipes created because of the author's love of food (She is a former chef.) and love for her children. If you are interested in how one mom tackles food issues with her kids, you'll enjoy this approach.
Rating: Very good

+Gerard, Alice. *Please Breast-feed Your Baby,* New York: The New American Library, Inc., 1970.
A positive approach to breast-feeding that includes information on how the breast makes milk, preparing for breastfeeding, and future of breast-feeding. Easy-to-follow, helpful suggestions.
Rating: Very good

+Goldbeck, Nikki. *As You Eat, So Your Baby Grows,* New York: Ceres Press, 1980.
This little 16 page booklet is a simple, straightforward guide for healthy pregnancies. Includes recommended daily dietary allowance, the importance of special nutrients, diet tips, and what not to eat.
Rating: Very good

+Gooch, Sandy. *If You Love Me, Don't Feed Me Junk*. Virginia: Reston Publishing Co., 1983.
Author's own health problems led to better diet. She explains and examine the benefits of a whole foods diet for growing children. Practical parental advice given in easy-to-understand language. Short recipe section at the end gets you started on a better food path.
Rating: Good

+Kamen, Betty and Kamen, Si. *Kids Are What They Eat*, New York: Arco Publishing, Inc. 1983.
A tour of better health for children through skits, charts, make believe family shopping trips, etc. Information is valid and easy to read. Recipes represent the transition from traditional American diet to a natural foods diet.
Rating: Good

+Kelly, Karen and Hopkins, Joan. *Tilda's Treat, A New Way to Eat*, Connecticut: Keats Publishing, Inc., 1975.

A fantastic children's story with recipes as part of the story. The authors use brown sugar. I substitute date sugar. This book can be read by mid-grade children (8-10) or by parents to their younger children.

Rating: Very good

+Kitzinger, Sheila. *The Experience of Breastfeeding*, New York: Penguin Books, 1979.

This book emphasizes breastfeeding as an experience that should be enjoyed by mother, baby, and father. Informative and sensitively written, breast-feeding is realistically described. This book is a must for parents-in-waiting.

Rating: Excellent

+La Leche League International. *The Womanly Art of Breastfeeding*, Illinois: La Leche League International, 1981.

Considered a classic among nursing mothers. This new 25th anniversary edition covers all aspects of breastfeeding. Included is helpful information on pre-birth care, fathering, solid foods, special problems, and the superiority of breastmilk.

Rating: Very good

+Larson, Gena. *Better Food for Better Babies*, Connecticut: Keats Publishing, Inc., 1972.

A two-part guide book for parents. First part gives nutritional information on pre-conception diet, pre-natal diet, nursing, infant feeding, and preschoolers' diet. Second half provides natural food recipes for infants, toddlers, and the whole family.

Rating: Very good

+McEntire, Patricia. *Mommy, I'm Hungry*, California: Cougar Books, 1982.

A fine collection of suggestions for getting and keeping your child on natural foods. Recipes use natural food ingredients but also mayonnaise, margarine, mustard, and a few ingredients I wouldn't consider wholesome.

Rating: Very good

*+Montagu, Ashley. *Life Before Birth*, New York: The New American Library, 1964.

Sensitive treatment of pregnancy. Includes information on nutrition, harmful influences (drugs, tobacco, x-rays), problems in pregnancy and delivery, and finally the actual birth. A must reading for all concerned parents-to-be.

Rating: Excellent

+Montgomery, Herb and Mary. *Rejoice! A Child is Born*, Minnesota: Winston Press, 1977.

A beautiful picture book for parents expressing thought on love, wonder, creativity, security, joy, and all the aspects that can make parenting as wonderful as life itself.

Rating: Excellent

+Raphael, Dana. *The Tender Gift: Breastfeeding*, New York, Schocken Books, 1977.

A different kind of book on breastfeeding, this emphasizes mothering the mother to make breastfeeding enjoyable and successful. Borrowing the "doula" concept from primitive cultures, she suggests we westernized parents set up our own doula system (mothers* support system in the form of parent, husband, friend) to ensure successful breastfeeding and positive transition into the state of motherhood.

Paring: Excellent

Reno, Tosca. *The Eat-Clean Diet for Family & Kids*. Ontario, Canada: Robert Kennedy Pub., 2008.

This visually appealing book filled with photos, charts, and colorful pages contains 14 topics of concern to parents, including Our Kids' Failing Health, Eating Out, In the School Cafeteria and Clean-eating Recipes (meals, sides and treats). Helpful tips throughout the book. Recipes require commitment to your kids' health.

Rating: Excellent

Sears, M., MD, Sears, M. RN, Sear,J. MD, Sears, R. MD. *The Healthiest Kids in the Neighborhood*. New York: Little Brown & Co. 2006. Website: www.searsparenting.com or www.AskDrSears.com.

This book is an idea whose time has come. Today's world of fast/fatty foods, junk food, questionable ingredients, etc. has made parenting wisely about food choices quite difficult. The 12 chapters cover a wide array of issues, including,: Feed Your Family the Right Carbs, Food Shopping with Your Kids, and healthful recipes. A no nonsense book by doctors and a nurse that reads easily with lists and images and boxes of information called Nutshells, such as "The greener the green, the more nutrients in them.

Rating: Very Good to Excellent

+Shandler, Michael and Nina. *The Complete Guide and Cookbook for Raising Your Child as a Vegetarian*, Schoken Books, New York, 1981.

Thorough guide for parents and parents-to-be who want a meatless diet for themselves and their offspring. This book has three parts—a nutrition guide, growth stages, and recipes. The cookbook part is divided into dairy and dairyless, and egg and eggless recipes made with wholesome ingredients sure to please even the most finicky of children, vegetarian or otherwise. Middle of the road vegetarianism is emphasized—no extreme diets like 7 macrobiotic or all-raw food. This is a basic vegetarian guidebook for parents.

Rating: Very good

+Shelton, Herbert. *Hygienic Care of Children*, Connecticut: Natural Hygiene Pres, 1970. (Revised edition now available.)

A fairly radical approach to bringing up children, this book is the natural antithesis to all other medical jargon on child-rearing. While I disagree with some of his ideas, most of the information makes sense once you accept natural hygiene; namely, the concept of supplying the body with basic requirements of nature: natural vegetarian diet, unpolluted air, exercise, rest, sleep, mental and emotional poise, wholesome environments, and productive activites.

Rating: Very good

*+Smith, Lendon, M.D. *Feed Your Kids Right*, New York: McGraw-Hill Book Company, 1979.

An excellent book on how food affects your child's behavior. Easy-to-read format. Includes a chapter on basic nutrients, supplements, and food to prevent future ailments. A modern Dr. Spock-type guidebook with emphasis on a natural diet for better mental and physical health.

Rating: Excellent

+Smith, Lendon, M.D. *Foods for Healthy Kids*, McGraw Hill Book Co., New York, St. Louis, et.al., 1981.

A perfect companion to Feed Your Kids Right, Dr. Smith has added recipes along with nutritional supplements for common and uncommon childhood ailments. Practical common sense suggestions and recipes combine to provide help for parents seeking good health through better nutrition.

Rating: Very good

*+Smith, Lendon, M.D. *Improving Your Child's Behavior Chemistry*, New York:

Simon and Schuster, 1976.

Deals with the relationship between food, child behavior, and health problems. Goes beyond the Feingold book, but is a little technical.

Rating: Good

+Wallace, Maureen and Wallace, Jim. *Snackers,* Washington: Madrona Publishers, Inc., 1978.

A snack book filled with recipes of every type. Most of their treats contain dairy or egg products. Substitutions can be made for children with allergies.

Rating: Very good

Weight Watchers. *Eat! Move! Play! A Parent's Guide for Raising Happy, Healthy Kids.* Hoboken, NJ: John Wiley & Sons, 2010.

A visually appealing book with colorful photos and layouts that covers Parenting Styles, Moving,& Playing, and Feeding Your Family. Strong message that diet and exercise are both important for parenting and cannot be left to chance.

Rating: Very Good

+Yntema, Sharon. *Vegetarian Baby*, New York: McBooks Press, 1980.

Extensively researched book on infant nutrition. Charts and recipes are valuable for both vegetarian and non-vegetarian baby diets. I disagree with her time table for introducing solids and mixing certain foods. Basically a good guide for feeding your baby (up to two years). Uses natural foods. Good bibliography.

Paring: Very good

+Zucker, Judi and Zucker, Shari. *How to Survive Snack Attacks Naturally,* California: Woodbridge Press Publishing Company, 1980.

A super beginner's snack book by teenage twins. Fun ingredients and simple recipes. Liberal uses of honey can be reduced. Uses no salt. Easy for kids to make themselves or with the help of an adult.

Rating: Very good

+Winick, Myron, M.D., *Growing Up Healthy*, William Morrow and Co., Inc. 1982.

Subdtled "A Parent's Guide to Good Nutrition," this comprehensive book by a nutrition-minded pediatrician covers common sense nutrition from pregnancy through adolescence. Easy to read with lay terms for the lay person.

Rating: Very good

G eneral Cookbooks

Note: The older titles that are still available are ones that guided me into healthier cooking. Hundreds of newer ones are available, many of the older ones have been updated, and I have included a few newer ones that I own, but I still rely on some of my old favorites available used online.

+Barkie, Karen E. *Sweet and Sugarfree,* St. Martin's Press, New York, 1982.
Some traditional and not-so-traditional dessert recipes, using fruit and fruit juice as the only sweeteners. Concept is good but should carry over to whole wheat flour instead of unbleached white, and low-calorie substitutions for high fat butter and cream cheese. Recipes for fruit sauces, puddings, jams, and frosty fruits are simpler and more wholesome.
Rating: Good

+Brown, Jo Giese. *The Good Food Compendium*, New York: Dolphin Books, 1981.
Comprehensive food book that successfully combines healthy foods with enjoyable eating. Charts, hints, food facts, and myths, and a large section on prenatal and children's diets. Excellent reference for good food enthusiasts plus tempting recipes.
Rating: Very good

+Cadwallader, Sharon. *Sharing in the Kitchen*, California: McGraw-Hill Book Company, 1979. (may be out of print)
Good beginners book for the single parent. Some questionable ingredients, yet, still within nutritious guidelines. Includes helpful hints.
Rating: Very good

Chesman, Andrea. *Serving Up the Harvest*. MA: Storey Publishing, 2005.
I love seasonal cookbooks, and this one even subdivides the seasons further, such as early to mid-summer and mid-to late summer. The cover notes that there are 175 simple recipes. But in addition to the recipes is background information on the basic foods to be used as well as introductory sections on the well-stocked pantry and mastering the basics.
Rating: Very good to excellent

+Claessens, Sharon. *The 20 Minute Natural Foods Cookbook*, Pennsylvania: Rodale Press, 1982.

This "quick-dish" cookbook is true to its title. Each dish is clocked to be ready in 20 minutes or less, but each dish is not a complete meal as the title implies. By combining two or three of Claessens' 20-minute dishes, you can prepare a complete meal in about one hour. The book is divided into three sections: Make It Fast; Make It Easy; Make It Ahead. Recipes are easy to read and to follow.

Rating: Very good

+Elliott, Sharon. *Busy People's Naturally Nutritious,* Decidedly Delicious Fast Foodbook, California: Fresh Press, 1977

Easy-to-make, quick, and wholesome cookbook whose complete title says it all. Food pictures are funky and recipes are simple. Good for kids who can read as well as adults who want good food fast.

Rating: Excellent

+Fisher, Bonnie. *Way With Herbs Cookbook,* Connecticut: Keats Publishing Inc., 1980.

A delightful cookbook emphasizing whole foods, with just a touch of herbs to enhance the true flavor of the recipes. Simple format, pleasant reading, tempting recipes.

Rating: Excellent

+Fishkin, Lois and DiMarco, Susan. *The Non-Strictly Vegetarian Cookbook,* Creative Arts Book Co., 833 Bancroft Way, Berkeley, CA 94710,1982.

A good transitional cookbook for those trying to reduce the family's meat intake. Oversized, hand-written pages make reading of recipes easy. It includes soups, salads, and desserts, as well as vegetarian, seafood, and chicken entrees. Does use salt and pepper, occasionally sugar, and a few other transitional ingredients.

Rating: Good to Very good

Note: Later editions available by Lois Dribin and Susan Ivanovich (1982 & 1995 –The New Not Strictly Vegetarian Cookbook)

+Greene, Diana Scesny. *Sunrise A Breakfast Cookbook Using Natural Foods And Whole Grains,* New York: The Crossing Press, 1980.

With this book, breakfast will never be boring. Using whole grains and natural toppings (fruit, nuts, yogurts), author Greene provides endless variations for whole grains breakfasts.

Rating: Very good

+Harrington, Geri. *The College Cookbook*, New York: Charles Scribner's Sons, 1973. updated 1988 by Don Harrington Associates.

Discusses eating off campus on a small budget. Author uses sugar. Recipes are fairly simple, use no exotic ingredient and emphasize unprocessed foods. Includes many helpful hints.

Rating: Good

+Johnson, Roberta Bishop, Ed. *Whole Foods for the Whole Family*, Illinois: La Leche League International Cookbook, 1981. Section for kids.

Considerable improvement from La Leche League's first cookbook. Good transitional book from traditional diet to natural diet. Includes cookbook section for kids; recipes without wheat, milk, or eggs; making your own yogurt; peanut butter and other staples; and information on tofu, sprouts, legumes, and grains. Detailed index makes this a most helpful book.

Rating: Very good

+Kinderlehrer, Jane. *Confessions of a Sneaky Organic Cook*, Pennsylvania: Rodale Press, Inc., 1971. Reissued by Newmarket Press in 1972.

A worthwhile book on food and health. Very readable. Includes food for teens and babies, a chapter of natural foods recipes (with and without meat), and information about weight loss. One of my earliest books to help me help my kids eat healthier.

Rating: Very good

Note: Jane Kinderlehrer, who was an editor at Prevention Magazine for 20 years, published a Smart Food Series, including Smart Muffins, all good choices when changing over to a healthier diet. Google her name for more health book titles by this author.

+Shell, Adeline Garner and Reynolds, Kay. Brown *Bagging It*, New York: Sovereign Books, 1979.

Small book filled with lunch bag ideas. Geared for both children and adults. Useful hints and innovative recipes.

Rating: Very good

Note: Shell also wrote *The Working Parent Food Book* (1979) Not rated.

+Stoner, Carol, Ed. The Natural Breakfast Book, Pennsylvania: Rodale Press, Inc.

Excellent source of good breakfast ideas. Recipes include making breads from whole grains, fruit and nut spreads, egg dishes, and natural, convenient breakfast foods. Dishes also suitable for meals other than breakfast.

Rating: Very good

Meatless Food Books

+Blanchet, Francoise, and Doornekamp, Rinke. *What to do with ...Vegetables,* Barren's Woodberry, New York, 1978. For kids.

A child's vegetable cookbook with 17 simple recipes using, for the most part, fresh ingredients. Simple, colorful illustrations that also serve to clarify instructions and to make recipes easy and attractive. Salt and pepper should be omitted and natural counterparts to commercial ingredients should be emphasized. Part of a series of four food books for children, although it can be used by adults or with adult supervision.

Rating: Fair to Good

+Brown, Edward Espe. *Tassajara Cooking,* California: Shambhala Publications, 1973.

Simple, unstructured, vegetarian recipes by a Zen Buddhist Often there are no specific amounts of ingredients. May be scary for the beginner or just what the novice needs. Does use salt, pepper, and sugar, but emphasis is on fresh, whole foods. Helpful information on cooking methods and utensils.

Rating: Very good

+Colbin, Annemarie. *The Natural Gourmet: Delicious Recipes for healthy, balanced eating.*

Annemarie Colbin started The Natural Gourmet Cookery School/Institute for Food and Health in 1997, where her healthy food philosophy are exemplified in her many books. This one is based on the Five Phases of Food, which is based on the Chinese concept of Wood, Fire, Earth, Metal, and Water, with corresponding foods, characteristics, seasons, and organs affected by these five points. A very interesting concept and cookbook, perhaps not for beginners, but certainly for anyone seeking a balanced, healthful diet.

Rating: Excellent

+Cottrell, Edyth Young. *Oats, Peas, Beans and Barley Cookbook*, California: Woodbridge Press, 1974.

A basic cookbook by a research nutritionist. Her recipes use the basic foods that help keep your food budget in line. While the book is vegetarian, the recipes and information are applicable for a natural food diet, with or without meat.

Rating: Very good

+Easterday, Kate Cusick. *The Peaceable Kitchen Cookbook*, New Jersey: Paulist Press, 1980.

Comprehensive beginner's whole food cookbook with full range of vegetarian recipes using eggs and dairy. The small amount of salt, pepper, brown sugar, and evaporated milk in some recipes can eventually be eliminated or substituted. Good definitions, easy-to-follow recipes, helpful how-to hints, nice layout, and graphics. An over-looked, but wonderful book for learning about whole foods.

Rating: Very good

+Ewald, Ellen Buchman. *Recipes for a Small Planet*, New York: Ballantine Books, 1973.

My first vegetarian cookbook. Based on the theory of complementary proteins; two non-meat foods properly combined will provide a complete protein. Recipes use milk, eggs, cheese, and wheat.

Rating: Good to Very good

+Ford, Frank. *The Simpler Life Cookbook*, Texas: Harvest Press, Inc. 1974. (Ford started Arrowhead Mills Natural Foods in Texas in 1960.)

Good cookbook using natural foods. Includes simple recipes for breads, breakfasts, soups, salads, vegetables, main dishes, and desserts. Emphasizes grains and beans. Also has information on camping foods and sources of natural foods.

Rating: Very good

+Goldbeck, Nikki and Goldbeck, David. *American Wholefoods Cuisine.* Woodstock, NY: Ceres Press. (New paperback edition 2006)

My cookbook "Bible," the one I turn to for basic recipes, like The Joy of Cooking, but for health food lovers. Subtitled: "More than 1300 meatless, wholesome Recipes from Short Order to Gourmet."

Rating: Excellent

+Goldbeck, Nikki and Goldbeck, David. *The Good Breakfast Book*, New York: Links Books, 1976.

A recipe-packed book of ideas, foods, and menus for a better breakfast. Includes cereals, dairy dishes, eggs, waffles, morning snacks, breads, and even soup for breakfast. Lots of good food and nutrition hints.

Rating: Very good

+Goldbeck, Nikki, *Cooking What Comes Naturally*, New York: Ceres Press, 1981.

A 30-day menu book for tasty vegetarian meals. Uses ethnic as well as traditional foods. Gives preparation time and helpful cooking hints. Good for beginning vegetarians and non-vegetarians looking for variety. Uses salt and pepper, but in small amounts.

Rating: Very good

Note: The Goldbecks have several wonderful books on a variety of topics. Google Ceres Press or their names for more information.

+Hoshijo, Kathy. *Kathy Cooks....Naturally.* San Francisco, CA: Harbor Publishing Inc., 1981.

More than 1,000 meatless recipes written in the spirit of self-sufficiency make this book an excellent introduction to natural foods. Tempting recipes are grouped under separate food divisions, for example, each chapter is about a different food, such as apples, potatoes, and legumes. The author's gourmet flair is marvelous, her philosophy admirable, and the nutritional information helpful. Even though some recipes use ingredients I avoid, such as salt and pepper, there are so many other recipes from which to choose that this fact is insignificant. This one book seems to have everything a beginner or veteran natural foods cook needs.

Rating: Excellent

Note: There are other vegetarian cookbooks by this author. Google her name.

+Jones, Dorothia Van Gundy. *The Soybean Cookbook*, New York: Arco Publishing Company, Inc., 1974

This cookbook emphasizes economical soy protein. Also includes history and nutritional value of the soybean, with recipes for this little-known, tasty food. Information on sprouting soybeans and various uses of soy products.

Rating: Very good

+Jordan, Julie. *Wings of Life*, New York: Crossing Press, 1976.

An unpretentious meatless cookbook whose aim is to "help you discover vegetarian cooking and develop your own style." Basic meat-free and natural food recipes include bread and spreads, grains, vegetables raw and cooked, soups, crepes, main dishes, and desserts. Does use salt and pepper in small amounts. Nice comments; homey.

Rating: Very good

+Katzen, Mollie. *The Enchanted Broccoli Forest*. Berkeley, CA: Ten Speed Press, 1982.

The author's second book, following on the heels of her ever-popular Moosewood Cookbook, emphasizes ethnic vegetarian dishes. Like the first book, it is hand lettered, recipes are quite lengthy and include salt, pepper, dairy and eggs. However, her reputation for tasty recipes stands firm.

Rating: Good

+Katzen, Mollie. *The Moosewood Cookbook*. Berkeley, CA. Ten Speed Press, 1977.

A large, hand-lettered, comprehensive cookbook based on recipes from The Moosewood Restaurant in Ithaca, New York. It contains vegetarian soups, salads, sandwiches, entrees, and desserts. Recipes use many ingredients as well as salt, pepper, dairy, and eggs. Good for transitional diet—moving from over-processed foods to natural foods. This book is considered one of the best of its kind.

Rating: Good

Note: Mollie Katzen has several newer cookbooks. Just Google her name for more information.

+Kloss, Jethor. The Back to Eden Cookbook, California: Back to Eden Books, 1974.

A vegetarian cookbook that uses soy products instead of eggs and cheese. May be helpful for allergy prone people. Helpful introduction on importance of whole foods.

Rating: Good to Very good

Note: Jethro Kloss' Back to Eden information book is considered a "Health Bible" by many people.

Landau, R. & Jacoby, Kate. Horizons Cookbook: Gourmet Meatless Cuisine. Tennessee: Book Publishing Company, 2003.

This wonderful cookbook is based on Horizons Restaurant in Philadelphia, which I live! While it is entitled a meatless cookbook, it is also a vegan cookbook, but even non-vegetarians will love the recipes, gathered from the co-authors many travels around the world to seek out cuisines that can be incorporated into their repertoire.

Excellent

Note: Horizons has a new cookbook, Horizons: New Vegan Cuisine, which is on my "must get" list. Also, check out their website: http://www.horizonsphiladelphia.com/

Lappe, Frances Moore. Diet for a Small Planet, New York: Ballantine Books, 1971. New edition; updated 1982.

More than a cookbook — a food book that explains complementary proteins in detail (this concept is played down in 10th anniversary edition). Recipe section covers foods for all your basic menu needs.

Rating: Excellent

Note: Lappe also started The Small Planet Institute. With daughter Anna, they continue to provide helpful information on food and the planet. (Ex. Anna Lappe has written Diet for a Hot Planet, where she explores the intersection between global climate change and the way we eat. (from their website: www.smallplanet.org.)

+Layne, Kendall. *Cooking for Consciousness,* Colorado: Ananda Marga Publications, 1976.

An egg-free cookbook published by a spiritual group. A large variety of recipes with information on eating habits, nutrition, "kitchen ways," canning and preserving.

Rating: Very good

Note: The updated 1993 version had an additional author: Joy McClure

*+Nearing, Helen. *Simple Food for the Good Life,* New York: Delacourte Press, 1980.

This book successfully combines recipes, a good food philosophy expressed through choice quotes from various books, and information on the value of fresh, whole fruits, nuts grains, seeds, and greens. More than a cookbook, this is a total reading experience that is sure to whet the appetite and give food for thought.

Rating: Excellent

+Norton, Reggi and Wagner, Martha. *The Soy of Cooking,* Eugene, Oregon: White Crane, 1981.

For those adventuresome cooks who want to try tofu (soybean curd) and tempeh (fermented soybean cake) recipes, this is the book for you. Salads, snacks, main dishes, and desserts, all using tofu or tempeh in creative ways.

Rating: Good to Very good

Patrick-Goudreau, Colleen. *The Vegan Table.* Beverly, MA: Fair Winds Press, 2009.

A well-organized and designed cookbook for all occasions. You won't even realize it's vegan! Recipes seasonal within different categories, such as Romantic Dinners for Two and Feasts for the Holidays. Sprinkled with food and nutrition tips and food lore.

Rating: Excellent

Note: Author also has a book called The Joy of Vegan Baking

+Phillips, Ann Vroom and Phillips, David A. *The Soil to Psyche Recipe Book,* California: Woodbridge Press Publishing Company, 1977.

Interesting meatless cookbook by an Australian. Recipes preceded by information on Australia and food uses. Author aim to expand new vegetarians' repertoire of established vegetables. Nutritional recipes with adventure.

Rating: Very good

+Robertson, Laurel; Hinders, Carol and Godfrey, Bronwen. *Laurel's Kitchen,* California: Nilgiri Press, 1976. (There is also The New Laurel's Cookbook, with Brian Ruppenthal instead of Bronwen Godfrey as an author. 1986: CA: Ten Speed Press.)

A comprehensive handbook on nutrition for vegetarians. Useful for all people interested in wholesome food. May be overwhelming for the beginner, but handy to have as a nutritional reference.

Rating; Very good

(Note: Laurel Robertson has several cookbooks. Google Laurel's Kitchen.)

Rovira, Eleanore, ed. *The What to do with Tofu Cookbooklet,* Philadelphia, Pennsylvania: The Grow-cery.

A thirty page booklet with simple recipes using tofu (soybean curd). Good book to use as an introduction to this food. Does use salt and pepper.

Rating: Good to Very good

Note: The Internet replaces this cookbook with a website: http://www.aloha-tofu.com/tofu_recipes.htm. Includes recipes and tofu products.

Quinn, Janie: *Essential Eating: Sprouted Baking.* Waverly, PA: Azure Publishing, 2008. This excellent book on baking with sprouted grains will become a favorite in your kitchen if you believe in the power of sprouts. The recipes are tasty and the book has beautiful photos of the food. Includes excellent information on the importance of sprouts and sprouted grains.

Rating: Very good to Excellent

Note: Other books by Quinn can be found on her website: essentialliving. com

+Shandler, Michael and Nina. *The Complete Guide and Cookbook for Raising Your Child as a Vegetarian.* Shocken Books, New York, 1981.

See description under Children's Diet section.

Silberstein, Susan, PhD. *Hungry for Health: 157 delicious, nutritious dishes to help prevent and reverse disease.* W. Conshohocken, PA: Infinity Publishing Co. 2008.

A wonderful cookbook with easy-to-make recipes including appetizers & snacks, soups & broths, salads & dressings, entrees & sides, sweets & treats, juices & smoothies. Recipes will appeal to kids and adults. Informative basic introduction and "health quotes" with each recipe page.

Rating: Excellent!

Note: Go to the website for more books and information on her organization: www.beatcancer.org.

Spivack, Ellen Sue. *Beginner's Guide to Meatless Casseroles.* Ross Books, Berkeley, 1984.

A compact, spiral-bound book full of delicious, simple, meatless recipes. Contains cooking hints and a glossary.

Rating: Very good

This was my first cookbook under my previous name and is available directly from me in photocopy form. Contact me at writeonthyme@yahoo.com.

+Thomas, Anna. *The Vegetarian Epicure*, New York: Vintage Books, 1972.

This highly acclaimed vegetarian, gourmet cookbook uses milk, butter, eggs, and brown sugar liberally. Food for a transitional natural foods diet, but these tempting dishes should eventually be used less frequently than simpler recipes.

Rating: Good

+Thomas, Anna. *The Vegetarian Epicure Book 2*, New York: Alfred Knopf, 1978.

This second book is based on cuisine from other countries and cultures. While she cooks from scratch, Thomas does use salt, sugar, cream, eggs, and hot spices liberally. Recipes are good for transitional gourmet seeking tasty vegetarian alternatives using familiar ingredients.

Rating: Good

Note: Author Ana Thomas has a website with more cookbooks and recipes: www.vegetarianepicure.com/

+Tracy, Michael. *The Mild Food Cookbook*, Utah: Dial Printing Service, 1975.

This small, recipe-packed cookbook is based on mucusless foods. Includes all fruits, green, leafy vegetables, and most other vegetables eaten by our Biblical ancestors. Meat, dairy products, white potatoes, eggs, rice, and other unsprouted grains are excluded. Great for children on special diets.

Rating: Excellent

Turner, Kristina. *The Self-Healing Cookbook: A Macrobiotic Primer for Healing Body, Mind, and Moods with Whole, Natural Foods.* Gras Valley, CA, Earthtones Press, 2002 (newer edition).

A helpful introduction to macrobiotics with charts, line drawings, and homey-like layout. A mixture of information and recipes, so it can be used a guide as well as a cookbook.

Rating: Very Good to Excellent

+Withim, Gloria. *Elegant Eating in Hard Times,* Trumensburg, New York: The Crossing Press, 1983.

If you think meatless cooking is dull, you haven't tried this cookbook. A graduate of Cordon Bleu in London, the author makes meatless dishes attractive for any palate. However, she does use lots of dairy, eggs, and spices which may move it from a health cookbook to a gourmet cookbook using fresh ingredients.

Rating: Good

+Zucker, Judi and Shari. *How to Eat Without Meat*, California: Woodbridge Press Publishing Company, 1981.

A companion to their successful first book How to Survive Snack Attacks. The double energy twins present a simple lacto-ova vegetarian cookbook for even the most timid beginner seeking a better diet, vegetarian or otherwise.

Rating: Very good

Sprouting and Raw Food Books

Note: International Specialty Supply has a website listing many, many books on cooking and especially sprouting books. I placed another + on those titles listed on the site. They do not sell them, but the list is a helpful bibliography.

Go to: http://www.sproutnet.com/sprouting_books.htm

Also, many other books on raw foods, juicing, herbs, etc. can be found at: http://www.therawfoodworld.com

++Acciardo, Marcia. *Light Eating for Survival*, Iowa: Twenty-First Century Publishing, 1978.

Comprehensive raw food book with many recipes to satisfy every palate. Contains information on "new age" foods and its positive tone indicates that eating uncooked foods is a pleasant and nourishing experience.

Rating: Excellent

Ananda, Sita. *Love the Sunshine in With Sprouts*. Oregon: Better Health for Life, 1982. Based on the concept of biogenics, which can be defined as germinated seeds, whle grains, nuts, legumes, and tender baby greens that have the biochemical capacity to mobilize their dormant life forces and thus create and generate new life. (From the inside cover) This is a simple, but comprehensive, guide to growing sprouts, including recipes, storing the seeds and beans for sprouting, and helpful charts.

Rating: Very good

++Blauer, Stephen. *The Miracle of Sprouting*, N.J. Avery Publishing Group, 1982.

Basic sprout book with easy directions. Clean recipes, simple, no cooking, tempting.

Rating: Excellent

+Courter, Gay. *The Beansprout Book*, New York: Simon &. Schuster, 1972.

My favorite book on sprouting. Contains directions, sketches, recipes, and ideas for sprouting in easy-to-read print, as well as a list of suppliers of sprouting seeds and beans.

Rating: Excellent

+Hunsberger, Eydie Mae and Loeffler, Chris. *Eydie Mae's Natural Recipes,* California: Production House Publishers, 1978.

Emphasis on raw foods. Author was cured of cancer with raw foods, and passes along terrific ideas for uncooked dishes. Recipes can please any palate.

Rating: Excellent

++Jensen, Dr. Bernard, D.C. *Seeds and Sprouts for Life,* California: Bernard Jen-sen Products.

A little 50-page booklet chock-full of facts about the nutritional value of sprouts and seeds. Contains descriptive, alphabetical listing of seed foods and their value, plus 10 pages of sample recipes.

Rating: Very good

*+Kulvinskas, Viktoras, M.S. *Love Your Body,* Iowa: Twenty-First Century Publishing, 1974.

Straightforward information on the importance of raw foods and sprouting for superior health. Easy recipes. Concepts considered radical by some, and the only way to eat by others.

Rating; Excellent

Meyerowitz, Steve. *The Kitchen Garden Cookbook.* MA: Sproutman Publications, Inc. As his website (www.sproutman.com) states, Sproutman Steve Meyerowitz is one of the world's leading proponents of sprouting, juicing, fasting, wheatgrass, indoor gardening, raw foods, and pure water. He was christened "Sproutman" in the 1970s because of his passion for sprouts and indoor gardening and the nutritious, organic foods they provide. The title above is only one of many on his website that reflects his knowledge of sprouting.

Rating: Very good to excellent

++Oliver, Martha H. *Add a Few Sprouts,* Connecticut: Keats Publishing, Inc., 1975.

Good all-around book on sprouts. Includes interesting information on history of sprouts, biochemical analysis, the how-to's of sprouts, and many recipes.

Rating: Very good

+Whyte, Karen Cross. *The Original Diet,* California: Troubador Press, 1977.

A guidebook on raw foods that includes interesting historical information about early man's diet. Uses a wide variety of sun-ripened, unfired (raw) foods.

Rating: Excellent

+Whyte, Karen Cross. *The Complete Sprouting Cookbook*, California: Troubador Press, 1973.

A good, basic, sprouting book with lots of sprout recipes. Includes how to buy or store different seeds and their uses with almost every type of food. Large recipe section.

Rating: Very good

M iscellaneous Books

Note: These are miscellaneous books that helped me navigate the nutrition waters early on and still help me. The older ones are still available through the Internet or used bookstores and newer ones on various health topics still are being published, so don't hesitate to do your own research for books on various topics.

+Brown, Edward Espe. *The Tassajara Bread Book*, Colorado: Shambhala, 1970.

A nice book for those interested in breadmaking. Detailed instructions and lots of recipes for yeasted and unyeasted bread, all with pleasant line drawings.

Rating: Good

+Clark, Linda. *Know Your Nutrition*, Connecticut: Keats Publishing Company, 1973.

Easy to read. Gives straightforward information on vitamins and minerals with a brief, informal chapter on high-powered foods.

Rating; Very good

+Dufty, William. *Sugar Blues*, Pennsylvania: Chilton Book Company, 1975.

An eye-opening account of sugar, starting back in Biblical times. Well-written and well-researched. Interesting reading.

Rating: Excellent

+Dworkin, Stan and Dworkin, Floss. *Blend it Splendid*, New York: Bantam Books, Inc., 1973

Imaginative recipes for the blender. Includes soups, dressings, beverages, desserts, and natural and dietetic candies. Emphasis is on minimal processing and cooking to preserve nutrients.

Rating: Very good

Goldbeck, Nikki & Goldbeck, David. *Healthy Highways.* Woodstock, New York: Ceres Press, 2009 (2nd edition). A great book to have in your glove compartment, because it guides you to healthy eateries all across the country, wherever you travel, with icons to tell you the type of eatery, cost, etc.
Rating: Excellent

+Gregory, Dick. Dick Gregory, *Natural Diet for Folks Who Eat*, New York: Harper and Row Publishers, 1973.
Personal account by ex-comedian and political vegetarian activist. Helpful information and interesting reading. Includes some menus and recipes for babies, weight conscious individuals, and pets.
Rating: Very good

+Hunter, Beatrice Trum. *How Safe is the Food in Your Kitchen?*, New York: Charles Scribner's Sons, 1981.
Straightforward data on safety of kitchen utensils, cooking equipment, and drinking water. Addresses for more information included where appropriate. Valuable kitchen guide for concerned consumer.
Rating: Very good

*+Hunter, Beatrice Trum. *The Natural Foods Primer*, New York: Simon &. Schuster, 1972.
The subtitle, "Help for the Bewildered Beginner," is the best description for this handy guide to natural foods. One of the first books I read when I began my quest for better foods in my family.
Rating: Excellent

+Hunter, Beatrice Trum. *Favorite Natural Foods,* New York: Simon &. Schuster, 1974.
This easy-to-read, well-documented book is based on a series of TV programs done by Ms. Hunter. Each chapter represents one basic natural foods concept with recipes. It includes vegetables, salads, whole grains, sauerkraut, yogurt, soybeans, desserts, and special concerns. Each chapter contains useful information on purchasing, storing, and preparing, as well as a mini-glossary of all items listed.
Rating: Very good
Note: Beatrice Trum Hunter has many more excellent books. Just Google her name for the list.

+Lasky, Michael. *The Complete Junk Food Book*. New York: McGraw Hill, 1977.

Author Lasky, a confessed junk food (ex) junkie, has done an outstanding job explaining the relationship between junk food and our health. A junk food almanac, a list of fast food restaurants with his ratings, plus a wonderful smattering of humor sprinkled throughout the text, make this a great guide for anyone who needs convincing that junk food is junk, no matter how well it is wrapped and advertised.

Rating: Excellent

Magazines & Newsletters with their Websites-Updated List

There are dozens of magazines and newsletters on the newsstands and online. Several are devoted only to food and health, while most major magazines now have health sections. This is just a small sample to get you going. I have not rated them, because each one deals with slightly different issues and they will be helpful at different stages of your change to a better eating plan. I have included only ones I have found helpful, in general. Many have free sample issues on their websites and some are with the subscription.

Concerning websites not linked with magazines or newsletters: There are hundreds of sites with hundreds of categories on food and health and fitness. Just type in your topic in the address box and several pages will come up for you to peruse. Don't get hung upon information overload. Pick a few sources and then check with your doctor or other health professional for his or her opinion.

Clean Eating. One year (12 issues) , $19.97. Ontario, Canada. Based on consuming food in its most natural state, or as close to it as possible. It's is not about just a diet, but about a lifestyle of improving you life---"one meal at a time.

Contatc: www.cleaneating.com or 1-905-507-3545 or 1-888-254-0767.

Cooking Light Magazine. Published monthly. Subscription $15. Claims to be the most popular cooking magazine in the USA. Mainstream recipes that are healthy counterparts to the standard American diet. (SAD). Contact: PO Box 62376, Tampa, FL, 33662-3768 or www.CookingLight.com.

Eating Well Magazine. Published 6 times per year for $15. Motto is: Where Good Taste Meets Good Health. Contact: 823A Ferry Rd. PO Box 1010, Charlotte, VT 05445 or www.eatingwell.com.

Health. 10 issues, $9.95. Their online ad reads: "Health features informative articles on how to stay fit, look great and feel fantastic."

Upbeat magazine that includes basic health issues, medical information, exercise, & recipes. Focus seems to be on making healthy "hip." Contact: www.health.com or 1-800-274-2522.

Health Science Magazine: Published quarterly. A $35 yearly membership fee in The National Health Association (NHA), which promotes the benefits of a plant-based diet, exercise and rest, a healthy environment, psychological well-being, and, when indicated, the use of fasting, includes a subscription to the magazine. Contact: Natural Health Association, PO Box 30603, Tampa, FL 33630 or www.healthscience.org

Living Without. Published 6 times per year for $23.. Motto is: Living Without is your guide to living with Allergies. Covers multiple allergy concerns and started by a woman with celiac disease. Contact: P.O. Box 420234
Palm Coast, FL 32142-0234 or www.livingwithout.com.

The Mother Earth News: published bimonthly. Price $3.00 per copy. Subscription rate: $15 per year. Foreign and Canada $17.00. Mail subscription orders and inquiries to: Mother Earth News, P.O. Box 70, Hendersonville, NC 28739.

Mothering: published quarterly. Price $2.75 per copy. Subscription rate: $10.00 per year. Foreign and Canada add $3.00 per year. Mail subscription orders and inquiries to: Mothering, P.O. Box 2046, Albuquerque, NM 87103.

Prevention Magazine: Published monthly. One of the earliest magazines on health and fitness; compact size. 12 issues for $11.88, Canada $15.97. Contact: 33 Minor St., Emmaus, PA 18098 or www.prevention.com/health.

Vegetarian Journal. Published quarterly. Subscription rate: $20 per yr. VRG Newsletter is free online at www.vrg.org."The practical magazine for those interested in Vegetarian Health, Ecology, and Ethics." Contact: Vegetarian Resource Group, PO Box 1463, Baltimore, MD. 21203 or www.vrg.org.

Vegetarian Times: 9 issues yearly for $14.95, Canada: $26.95, International $38.95. One of or maybe, the first vegetarian magazines. Contact: 888-590-0030 or www.vegetariantimes.com.

Environmental Nutrition. $39 for 12 issues yr. Slim newsletter packed with nutritional information to help consumers make knowledgeable choices about their health. Contact PO Box 420235, Palm Coast, FL 32142-0235 or www.

environmentalnutrition.com.

Food First. Published by Institute for Food & Development Policy. Membership of $40 entitles you to quarterly publications or print out at the website, www.foodfirst.org. This non-profit institute was founded in 1975 by Frances Moore Lappe and Joseph Collins. As a public education center it investigates "the causes of hunger in a world of plenty. Contact: 398 60th St., Oakland. CA, 94618 or website.

La Leche League. Several publications available. Message on website: "Get breastfeeding help, learn about breastfeeding and the law, find resources for health care providers or Leader and more." Contact: La Leche League International, PO Box 4079, Schaumburg, IL 60168-4079 or www.llli.org. or 847-519-7730.

Nutrition Action Magazine. Published by Center for Science in the Public Interest (CSPI). 10 issues yearly for $24. Actually a mini-magazine rather than a newsletter, publication covers current issues on health, written provocatively to keep your interest. "Politics of food" could be the subtitle, although recipes, charts from CSPI, and special sections (e.g. Food Porn) make it a well-rounded food publication. Contact: CSPI, 1875 Conn, Ave., NW, Washington, DC, 20009 or www.cspinet.org.

The People's Doctor Newsletter written by Dr. Robert Mendelsohn, a well-known doctor in the nutrition field subtitled: "A Medical Newsletter for Consumers." After his death, the magazine became known as The Doctor's People and archives the newsletters at: http://www.accessmylibrary.com/archive/412268-the-doctors-people-newsletter.html. Also, Google the doctor's name for the excellent books he wrote.

Pure Facts, Feingold Association of the United States.
Original newsletter based on Dr. Feingold's findings on hyperactivity, "based on the elimination of synthetic colors, synthetic flavors, BHA, BHT, TBHQ, and naturally occurring salicylates from our food supply." Online newsletter expands the information to include autism, depression, eczema, sleep disorders, etc. Contact: www.feingold.org or 1-800-321-3287.

Vegetarian Voice, published by North American Vegetarian Society (NAVS). Subscription: $22 for individual membership, 28 for family membership. Includes 40 recipe cards and helpful booklet on vegetarianism. Free online newsletter. Contact: P.O. Box 72, Dodgeville, NY 13329 or www.mans-onbline.com

Glossary

Amaranth — A newly rediscovered plant high in protein calcium and fiber used in baking and cooking. Suitable for grain-free diets.

Autism — Condition in which one operates entirely by internal stimuli and tunes out the world around him/her.

Arrowroot Starch — A fine, powdery, white substance used like cornstarch in cooking. Easily digested. Good for people allergic to corn or potato starch.

Barley — (hulless or whole hulled) one of the oldest cultivated grains; when pearled, as is the usual form, the nutritious bran coating, containing the B vitamins, is lost.

Barley/Malt Syrup — A liquid sweetener made from sprouted barley grains; not as sweet as honey, but has a smooth taste. Use sparingly.

BHA, BHT — Synthetic antioxidants used to prevent oxidation of oils. Considered hazardous.

Bran — The outer part of the wheat kernel, which remains intact in whole wheat flour but is removed when grain is milled into white flour. Contains vital nutrients, especially B vitamins, and is a high fiber source.

Buckwheat — Not a true grain like wheat, since the fruit, and not the seeds, of the plant are eaten. It is used like a grain. More commonly known as kasha.

Bulghur — A toasted cracked wheat that still has the bran and germ of the grain but in a roasted and cracked form, which may be considered less nutritious by some. Popular in the Middle East, where they use it to prepare a cold grain salad called tabouli.

Carob — A dark powder made from ground pods. Used as a chocolate substitute. High in minerals and, unlike chocolate, contains no caffeine or sugar when in its pure state. Also a good source of fiber, but should be used sparingly for infants because it contains tannic acid.

Clay — The fine powder of the Earth's crust. Used for its healing qualities and for cosmetics.

Corn Germ — The germ of the corn kernel; contains more fiber than wheat germ.

Couscous — A grain, as well as a dish, made from hard wheat, but not considered a whole grain. When cooked, it is light and fluffy, with a sweet grain taste.

Durum Wheat — Hard wheat used in making pasta; high in gluten and protein. Durum semolina is the name found on most pasta boxes. (See semolina.) Whole grain durum is preferred for healthier pasta.

Date Sugar — A granular sweetener made from dried dates that have been coarsely ground. Since ground dates are not a sugar extract or a highly refined product, some consider it a superior sweetener.

Emulsifier — Generally refers to a synthetic chemical used as a substitute for natural shortenings. When used in bread products, it makes the product softer and increases shelf life. Considered highly suspect. (Liquid lecithin is an alternative natural emulsifier.)

Familia — A breakfast cereal blend of raw, crushed, or flaked oats, nuts, dried fruit, fresh fruit, and often some other flaked grains, such as millet. Similar to an uncooked granola but not as sweet.

Fertile Eggs — Eggs from hens kept where there is an active rooster in the yard. The feed contains no chemicals, and the chickens roam freely, laying their eggs at will.

Fruit Butter — Natural spread made from fresh or dried fruit that has been cooked down to a "sauce" and pureed.

Graham Hour — A whole wheat flour named after Sylvester Graham, an early leader in the field of dietary reform. There is usually more bran in this flour, giving it a coarser texture.

Granola — A cereal made from flaked oats and often other whole grains, oven-toasted with honey or other liquid sweetener, oil, nuts, dried fruit, wheat germ, etc. Can also be used as a snack, as a topping for desserts, or as an ingredient in baked goods.

Honey — Natural sweetener produced from bees; best purchased in low heat and unfiltered form. Use sparingly; it is still a sugar.

Hydrogenated Oils — Oils treated with hydrogen to change their molecular structure so that their fat content is no longer digestible. Margarine is made solid through hydrogenation.

Hyperactivity — A loosely defined catch-all term, technically called hyperkinesis. Defines children showing excessive physical activity, along with problems of concentration and learning difficulties.

Instant Protein Drink — Highly processed powder, mainly made from soy beans or milk powder. Used to give a boost to drinks and other foods. Use occasionally.

Kefir — A fermented milk, somewhat like yogurt but made without heat or temperature control. The bacteria in kefir works to clear away unfriendly intestinal bacteria. Not as tart as yogurt.

Kelp — Type of seaweed used as a salt substitute when dried and powdered; high in iodine.

Lecithin (liquid) — An extract usually taken from soybeans. Used as a natural emulsifier and a natural preservative. Works very well alone or combined with oil to coat bake pans. Reduces cholesterol levels in the body.

Legume — The food category of beans, peas, and lentils. Legumes are inexpensive form of protein, as well as calcium and iron. Sometimes referred to as pulses.

Millet — A highly nutritious grain. Can be used at breakfast, dinner, or ground into flour for baking needs. Good source of non-gluten grain for those on a gluten-free diet.

Miso — Seasoning paste made from aged and fermented soybeans, barley, or rice, plus sea salt and water. Adds a hearty flavor to dishes. Used originally in the Orient, it is now a popular item in the western world.

Miso-Cup™ — The commercial form of powdered Miso. Used to flavor soups, salads, and casseroles. Dissolves more easily in water than Miso paste. (Available from Edwards &. Sons.)

Molasses — Thick, dark, strong-tasting syrup remaining in the "bottom of the barrel" when sugar cane juice is boiled down. Blackstrap is the first extraction from the bottom and considered highest in nutrients, especially iron. Use sparingly.

Natural Foods — General term used to describe foods that have not been refined and are still in their natural state, for instance, peanuts, unsprayed in unbleached shells.

Naturopath — A doctor who treats the whole body with a nutrition-oriented focus: encourages the body to heal itself, using fasting, rest, herbs, exercise, and a pure diet.

Nut Butter — Spread made from nuts, the most common being peanut butter; others are almond butter, cashew butter, and sesame butter or tahini; made from raw seeds.

Nutritional Yeast — A natural food supplement that is actually tiny living plants present in the air. Made commercially by growing the yeast in special mediums. A source of energy, derived from the B complex vitamins that are found in high doses in yeast. Brewer's yeast, a by-product of brewing, is the most familiar type, although there are other better tasting and higher nutrient level yeasts available. Not to be confused with baking yeast, which is used to make bread rise.

Organic Foods — Foods that have been grown on nutrient balanced soil, free of pesticides or artificial soil enrichment.

Polyunsaturated Oils — Refers to vegetable oils that are not saturated, that is, oils that can carry the fat soluble vitamins through the bloodstream, as well as perform other important bodily functions that animal fats cannot. Most common types: corn, peanut, safflower, sunflower, and sesame oil.

Raw Milk — Milk from cows or goats that has not been pasteurized or homogenized. Usually needs to be certified in order to be purchased commercially.

Salicylates — Group of compounds found naturally in a number of fruits and vegetables, which must be eliminated when treating hyperactivity, then replaced one food at a time to test for sensitivity.

Sea Salt — Salt from the evaporation of sea water. Higher in trace mineral than land minced sodium chloride (common table salt).

Semolina — The hard, durable part of the wheat grain used for making pasta and made from durum wheat.

Sorghum — Syrup extracted from the stalks of the sorghum plant. While it does not contain the high nutrition level of black strap molasses, it is less strong-tasting, closer to the flavor of barley/malt syrup.

Soy Sauce — A liquid extract made mainly from fermented soy beans. Also known as tamari or shoyu. Commercial soy sauce is not a fermented product and generally contains a preservative.

Sprouts — Seeds, beans and grains grown using water, not soil. When sprouted to maturity (3-5 days), they can be eaten in salads, sandwiches, casseroles, etc.

Tahini — Paste or spread made from raw, ground sesame seeds. If seeds are roasted, it is generally called sesame butter.

Tannic Acid — Powdered or flaked substance made from the bark and fruit of many plants. Used to tan leather and as an astringent.

Tofu — Curdled soy bean milk with a soft, bland, cheese-like consistency. Also known as bean curd. Originated in the Orient. An easily-digested, inexpensive source of high quality protein.

Triticale — A hybrid grain obtained from crossing wheat with rye. Higher in essential amino acids (protein building blocks) than either wheat or rye. Used like wheat or rye in cooking, baking, or sprouting.

Turbinado Sugar — Another term meaning raw sugar; unbleached.

Wheat Germ — The embryo of the wheat kernel, containing the vital nutrients lost when grains are milled into white flour. Can be raw or toasted, but both should be refrigerated at all times to retard rancidity.

Whole Wheat Berries — Another term for whole wheat grains that contain the kernels or berries with bran and wheat germ intact. Usually ground into flour for baking, or used whole for sprouting.

www.ingramcontent.com/pod-product-compliance
Lightning Source LLC
LaVergne TN
LVHW061223060426
835509LV00012B/1405